Musée Picasso

Cover illustration:
Mother and Child (detail), summer 1907.

Back cover illustration:
Le Déjeuner sur l'herbe, after Manet (detail), March-August

ISBN: 2-7118-4252-5

Musée Picasso

Marie-Laure Bernadac
Conservateur en chef du Patrimoine,
chargée de mission au musée Picasso

Réunion
des Musées
Nationaux

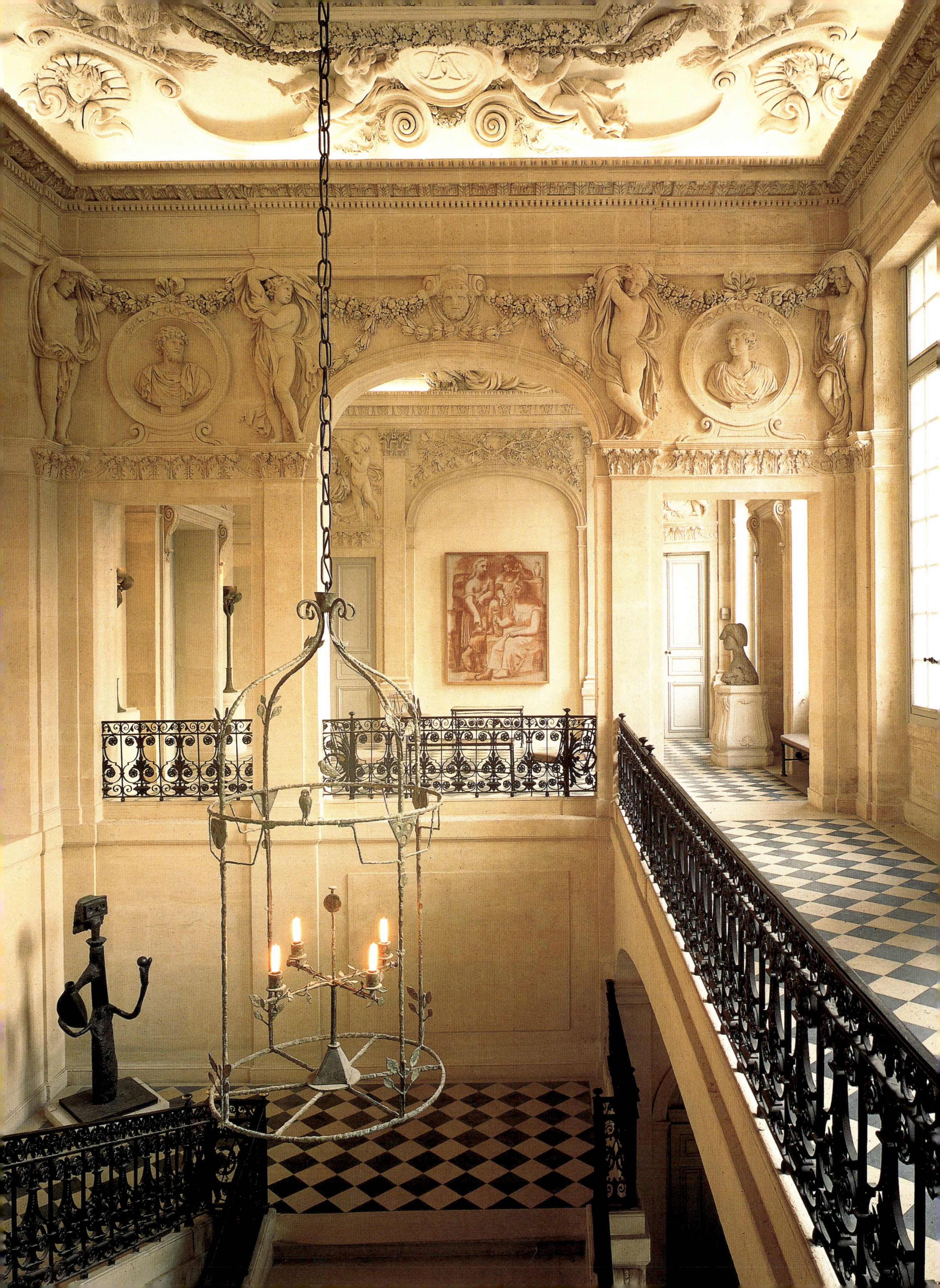

Marie-Laure Bernadac

Introduction

Pablo Picasso is probably the only artist of his time who fully justifies the creation of a monographic museum, entirely dedicated to his art and life. Not only the sheer quantity of works, due both to his longevity and his indefatigable and incessant output, but also the diversity of the techniques he used – painting, sculpture, engraving, drawing, ceramics, poetry – and, lastly, yet most importantly, the fact that, throughout his life, he refused to part with key works from each period, gave rise to the idea of assembling this collection in one place, a single museum that could epitomize the outstanding dimension of Picasso's universe. A museum that encompasses Picasso the artist, but also Picasso the man, as in his case, life and work were inseparable. His close and friendly relationships with the great creative people of his era (poets, writers, musicians, photographers, dancers), his incursions into other artistic fields (theatre, ballet, photography, film, poetry) and his involvement in historic events are just some of the many sides of Picasso's protean genius. He was the descendant of the great Renaissance masters, such as Michelangelo and Leonardo da Vinci, who cannot be defined merely as painters, sculptors or artists, for through their work, their knowledge and their way of thinking, they acquired a prophetic vision of the world, verging on the founding myths of mankind. They were not only the living incarnation of their era, but also universal geniuses.

The idea of the museum

Picasso seems to have always – perhaps unwittingly – had the idea of a museum. In fact, throughout his career, the way in which he built up a collection of Old Masters, tribal arts, contemporary works by fellow painters and even his own pictures, since he occasionally bought them back, proved that he was particularly fond of assembling and conserving this collection. "What is a painter at heart?" he used to say. "A collector who wants to build up a collection by painting the pictures he likes in other people's homes."[1] Furthermore, the interest he took in art from past eras, his regular visits to the Louvre, his admiration for the paintings he saw in museums and his obsessive desire to keep everything all show that he regarded museums as sources of aesthetic enjoyment, as the storehouses of memories and as the instruments through which one learned about art. Even if he once quipped, "Museums are full of lies; most of the people who specialize in art are imposters."[2] But what he was condemning at this point was narrow-minded conservatism, academic beauty, mausoleums, official art...

1. Daniel-Henry Kahnweiler, "Huit entretiens avec Picasso" in *Le Point*, October 1952.

2. Christian Zervos, "Conversations avec Picasso", in *Les Cahiers d'art*, 1935, pp. 173-178.

The creation of the Musée Picasso, Paris

Pablo Picasso died intestate, leaving an immense legacy of thousands of works. The dation law, enabling the heirs to pay their death duties in works of art, thus initiated the creation of this museum. Who were Picasso's heirs?

Maya, Marie-Thérèse Walter's daughter, Claude and Paloma, Françoise Gilot's children, Marina and Bernard, Paulo Picasso's children, hence the artist's grandchildren, and Catherine Hutin, Jacqueline Picasso's daughter. Thanks to the insight and generosity of all these heirs, and counter to the law, the French State was able to choose the works they would take in lieu of payment. Curator Dominique Bozo was put in charge of the huge and delicate task of selecting the works best suited to forming the museum collection from the thousands of pieces Picasso left behind. He was helped and advised by a group of Picasso's friends and art historians, including Jean Leymarie, Roland Penrose and Pierre Daix. His choice was governed by various criteria: to provide an overview of the artist's career covering all periods and all techniques; to introduce the public to little-known aspects of his oeuvre, long jealously guarded by the artist; to highlight the preparatory studies, the series, and, naturally, to give priority to "masterpieces". This initial dation, made in 1979, was composed of 203 paintings, 158 sculptures, 29 relief-paintings, 16 *papiers collés*, 88 ceramics, over 3,000 drawings and engravings, 34 sketchbooks, illustrated books and manuscripts, as well as works by other artists and some examples of tribal art.

Picasso's personal collection, which included key works by Paul Cézanne, Henri Matisse, Georges Braque, André Derain and Henri Rousseau, had previously been donated to the Louvre, in 1973. From 1979 onwards, it was transferred to the Musée Picasso, to complement the permanent collection there, by recalling the painter's own aesthetic world, his masters and his friends.

Since the foundation of the museum, further acquisitions and donations have enriched the collection. The most recent and most spectacular among them should be mentioned: *Three Figures under a Tree* (1908), a gift of William MacCarthy Cooper, Douglas Cooper's heir, *Celestina* (1904), a major work from the Blue Period, and *Dora and the Minotaur* (1936).

The Hôtel Salé

Finding a building worthy of housing such a collection and well-suited to the painter's temperament was the next task. The list of Picasso's various studios – the Château de Boisgeloup, the Hôtel des Grands-Augustins, Paris, the villa "La Californie", Cannes, the Château de Vauvenargues, the farmhouse "Notre-Dame-de-Vie", Mougins, – all testify to his pronounced taste for monumental old houses. The choice of a 17th-century mansion in the heart of Paris as a final place of residence to house his museum seemed perfectly obvious.

The second dation

Wealth, however great, begets wealth. Eleven years after the first dation, a second dation – smaller in quantity but just as moving and exciting – enriched the Musée Picasso's collection. In fact, after the tragic death of the painter's second and last wife, Jacqueline Picasso, on 15 October 1986, her daughter,

Catherine Hutin, in accordance with the law, offered the State a new group of works in partial payment of death duties. The final choice of works, consisting of 47 paintings, 2 sculptures, 40 drawings, 24 sketchbooks, 19 ceramics, 245 engravings and lithographs, considerably enriched the French national collections. In addition to the Picassos, there was a collage by Braque, one of the Cubist masterpieces, *Tivoli-Cinema* (1913). Much of this dation went to the Musée Picasso, to fill in the gaps or complete the groups in the existing collection. But an equally substantial part went to regional museums, such as the Musée Picasso, Antibes, and to the Centre Georges-Pompidou, Paris.

Picasso today

Even today, Picasso remains the best-known, and hence the least-known, artist of the 20th-century. It was as if his celebrity, the quasi-mythical aura surrounding him – founded on his immense wealth and his numerous love affairs – prevented people from seeing his work. The opening of the Musée Picasso in September 1985 was thus a cultural event of the utmost importance. Connoisseurs and neophytes could henceforth judge the exhibits for themselves, shake off prejudices that distorted their vision of his oeuvre, and learn how to look at, understand, and why not love it. For a very long time, the name Picasso was – and still is for some – the symbol of modern art, and even assumed a pejorative connotation: "That's very Picasso," people would exclaim in front of a picture whose meaning could not be instantly grasped. The bringing together and hanging of this collection introduces museum-goers to several artists in one; visitors thereby move from Picasso the Cubist to Picasso the Surrealist, from revolutionary Picasso to classical Picasso, from comedy to tragedy..., exploring each of the paths embarked upon by this elusive personality, this two-faced Janus inspired, in turn, by Apollo and Dionysus. Presented in a maze-like circuit with multiple entrances and exits, his works are either ahead of their time or revivals of former themes; these exhibition rooms provide one of the possible clues to the mystery of creation.

Each generation has its own vision of Picasso. Long ago, there was a preference for Picasso the Cubist and for his rigorous formal inventiveness, which played such a decisive role in future 20th-century art. Then there was the mediagenic Picasso the Communist, the committed Picasso, the painter of *Guernica*. Lastly, there was the misunderstood Picasso of the final period, only reinstated in its vivid topicality a decade ago through its resonance with contemporary painting. Major exhibitions dedicated to 1920s' Realism paid tribute to Picasso's classicist works. Today, thanks to the particularity of the museum collection, the public can discover a Picasso *furioso*, on the fringe of Surrealism, whose poetic, erotic and passionate universe constitutes one of the most powerful creative forces of all time. Picasso was the pivot, the unavoidable hub of all 20th-century artistic invention. There is scarcely any field of creation in which he did not make an impact. His work lives on, for it can be constantly rediscovered; it provides a lesson not only in art but also in enthusiasm and humanity.

The Death of Casagemas

Summer 1901, Paris

Oil on wood

27 x 35 cm

MP 3

In May 1901, Picasso visited Paris for the second time. He moved into the studio at 130, Boulevard de Clichy (9th arrondissement), inhabited a few months previously by his friend Carlos Casagemas, who had committed suicide there after an unhappy love affair. Haunted by this untimely death, the artist produced a series of posthumous portraits and drawings, including the famous *Burial of Casagemas* (1901, Musée d'Art Moderne de la Ville de Paris). In the painting here, the deceased is wrapped in a shroud, and only his face tinged with green is visible amidst the whiteness. The blackish mark made by the impact of the bullet can still be seen on his temple. Breaking the diagonal movement, a huge, vertical candle flame illuminates the painting. The candle radiating light – symbol of the passage of time and life's uncertainty – would reappear in the still lifes of the war years. The light falls on the shroud in yellow patches and outlines the deceased's profile. Vincent van Gogh's influence is evident; it can be seen in the broken brushwork on the light beams and the use of red, greenish-yellow and blue impasto.

"It was with the death of Casagemas in mind that I began to paint in blue,"[1] the artist later admitted to Pierre Daix. In fact, his friend's suicide brought about a dramatic transformation in Picasso's painting, which moved from the pre-Fauvist style seen in the exhibition at Ambroise Vollard's gallery, in June, to the monochrome pictures of the Blue Period.

1. Pierre Daix, *La Vie de peintre de Pablo Picasso,* Paris, Le Seuil, 1977, p. 47.

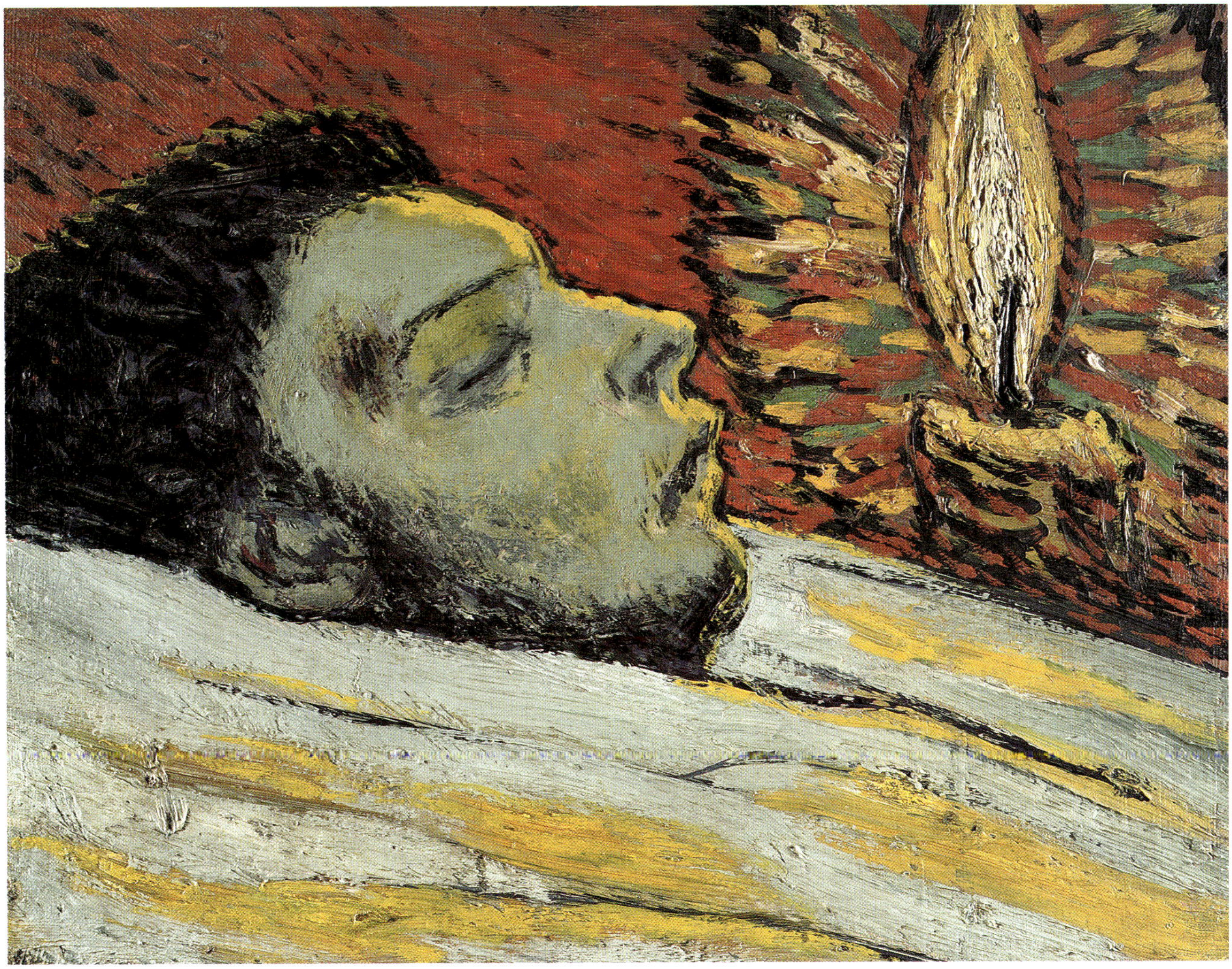

Self-Portrait

Late 1901, Paris

Oil on canvas

81 x 60 cm

MP 4

At once the image of a man and the subjective projection of the artist's vision, the self-portrait genre is doubly significant by its very nature. Painted in the winter of 1901, during Picasso's second visit to Paris, this self-portrait which marked the beginning of the Blue Period was the last in a series of similar works before Picasso returned to Barcelona, in January 1902.

At the time Picasso was only twenty years old, but in this image of himself he has aged considerably – the harsh winter has left him with an emaciated, hollow-cheeked face; his ashen complexion, highlighted only by pale pink lips, his bushy beard and hunched-up appearance in a heavy overcoat with upturned collar all emphasize the impression of sadness, poverty and solitude which emanates from this painting. The fluid lines of the coat and its handling in flat areas of monochrome blue, separated by a black contour, recall the influence of Henri de Toulouse-Lautrec and Paul Gauguin. The psychological intensity of the artist's sombre, quasi-hallucinated gaze is reminiscent of some of the self-portraits by Vincent van Gogh, who also influenced Picasso at this time.

This whole period is governed by melancholy. "The sterile sadness that overshadows the work of this very young man is extraordinary... Could this frighteningly precocious child be destined to consecrate a masterpiece to the negative side of life, to this pain from which he suffers more than any other?"[1] Blue is the colour of the night, "of moonlight, of water, blue of the Tuat in the Egyptian afterworld,"[2] wrote Carl Jung. But this monochromy also has formal repercussions, such as the simplification, stylization and unification of the composition. In fact, his use of blue does not merely mean wretchedness or hunger: "It asserts," wrote Alberto Moravia, "Picasso's determination to highlight his own, generic vitality, without making a judgment, without making a moral choice, through a totalitarian, demiurgic colour."[3]

1. Charles Morice, in *Mercure de France*, Paris, December 1902.
2. Carl Jung, "Picasso", in *Neue Zürcher Zeitung*, 13 November 1932.
3. Alberto Moravia, "Explosion de la manière", in *Tout l'oeuvre peint de Picasso, périodes bleue et rose*, Paris, Flammarion, 1980, p. 7.

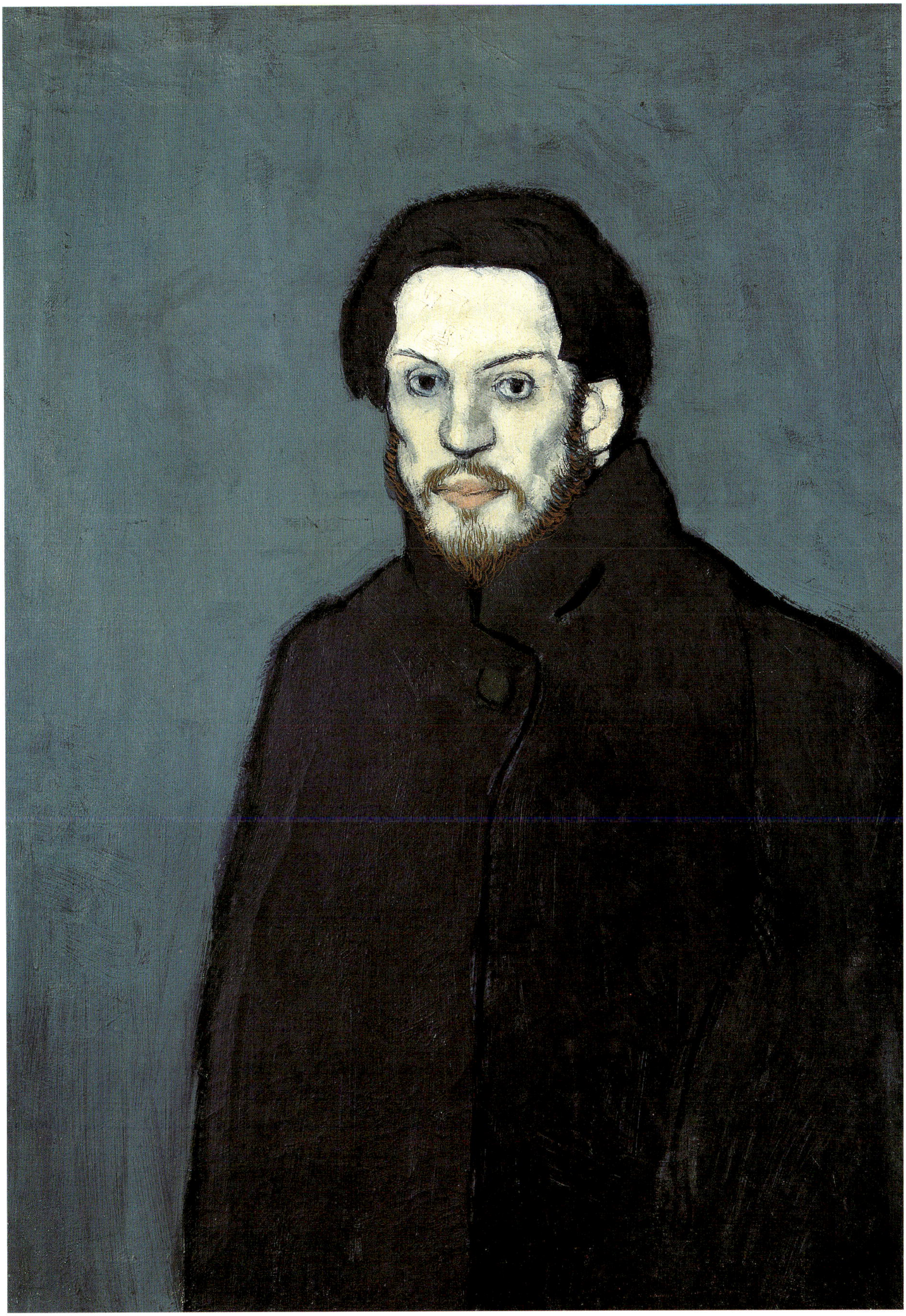

The Two Brothers

Summer 1906, Gósol

Gouache on cardboard

80 x 59 cm

MP 7

In the summer of 1906, Picasso and his companion Fernande Olivier left Paris for Gósol, a small village in the hills of Catalonia. This journey marked a new stage in his creative activity, bringing to fruition the profound change whose seeds had already been sown in 1905 with *The Family of Saltimbanques* (Washington, National Gallery of Art).

The painter abandoned the sentimental and literary aesthetics of the Blue Period – emaciated faces, images of distress and solitude – for a world of beauty, harmony and serenity. While the theme of the two young boys with finely drawn faces and pensive expressions full of brotherly love and the presence of the drum still evoke the world of the circus, on the contrary, the handling of the nude bodies in full, rounded volumes, the well-balanced, stable frontal pose and the warm ochre, greyish-blue and pink tones announce the new "classical" style Picasso explored in Gósol. The influence of ancient Greek statuary can already be seen in the stylized treatment of the legs and torso. Picasso combines the nude figure of the young ephebus not only with still-life elements – clay bowl and vase of flowers – and rhythmic devices, but also Mediterranean motifs that allude to the simple, rustic and bucolic life he was leading with Fernande in Gósol.

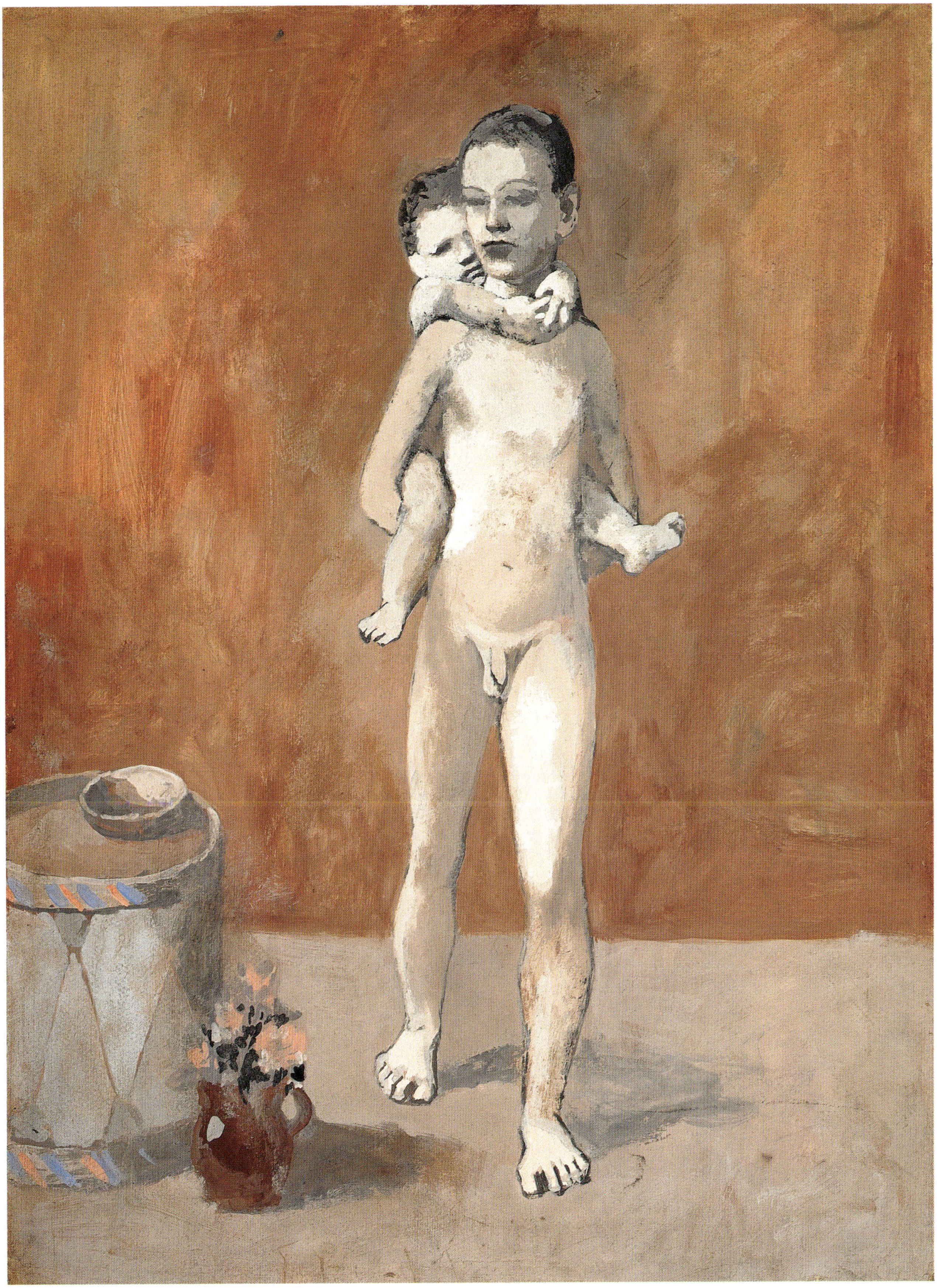

Self-Portrait

Autumn 1906, Paris

Oil on canvas

65 x 54 cm

MP 8

Representative of the final stage in the Gósol period, this self-portrait belongs to a series that includes, in addition to the *Self-Portrait with Palette* (Philadelphia, Philadelphia Museum of Art), also executed in 1906, numerous drawings, occasionally superimposed on the same sheet, in which Picasso used his own face to explore the mask device.

The torso is handled like architecture, the neck like a cylinder. The oval-shaped head appears to have been placed on a broad, stocky, robust trunk, which stems as much from the influence of Paul Cézanne's *Bathers* as from the painter's own particular morphology. The face, eyebrows, triangular nose and heavily outlined eyelids characteristic of the Gósol period and ancient Iberian statuary recur again here. However, in this portrait, the eyelids open to reveal the artist's sombre, fixed gaze. The asymmetrical treatment of the forehead not only enhances the gaze mysteriously, but somehow also heralds the dual viewpoints – frontal and in profile – the painter would subsequently adopt.

After the Rose Period, Picasso went back to using dull, greyish tones. The dense medium has been applied thickly and laboriously; the brushwork seems to carve out and build up the forms. Everything contributes to creating an impression of strength, solidity and serenity. It seems as if the body will be incapable of resisting this tension pumping up the volumes, this vital force hardening the muscles beneath the skin, for any length of time.

But what is most interesting about this painting is the depth and keenness of the gaze. The gaze is, in fact, a fundamental key to Picasso's work: changes in perception, the primacy of what is visible, his vision of the world and of himself, an open or closed window, the questions posed by the spectator – all that is expressed in the dark pupils of Picasso's eyes.

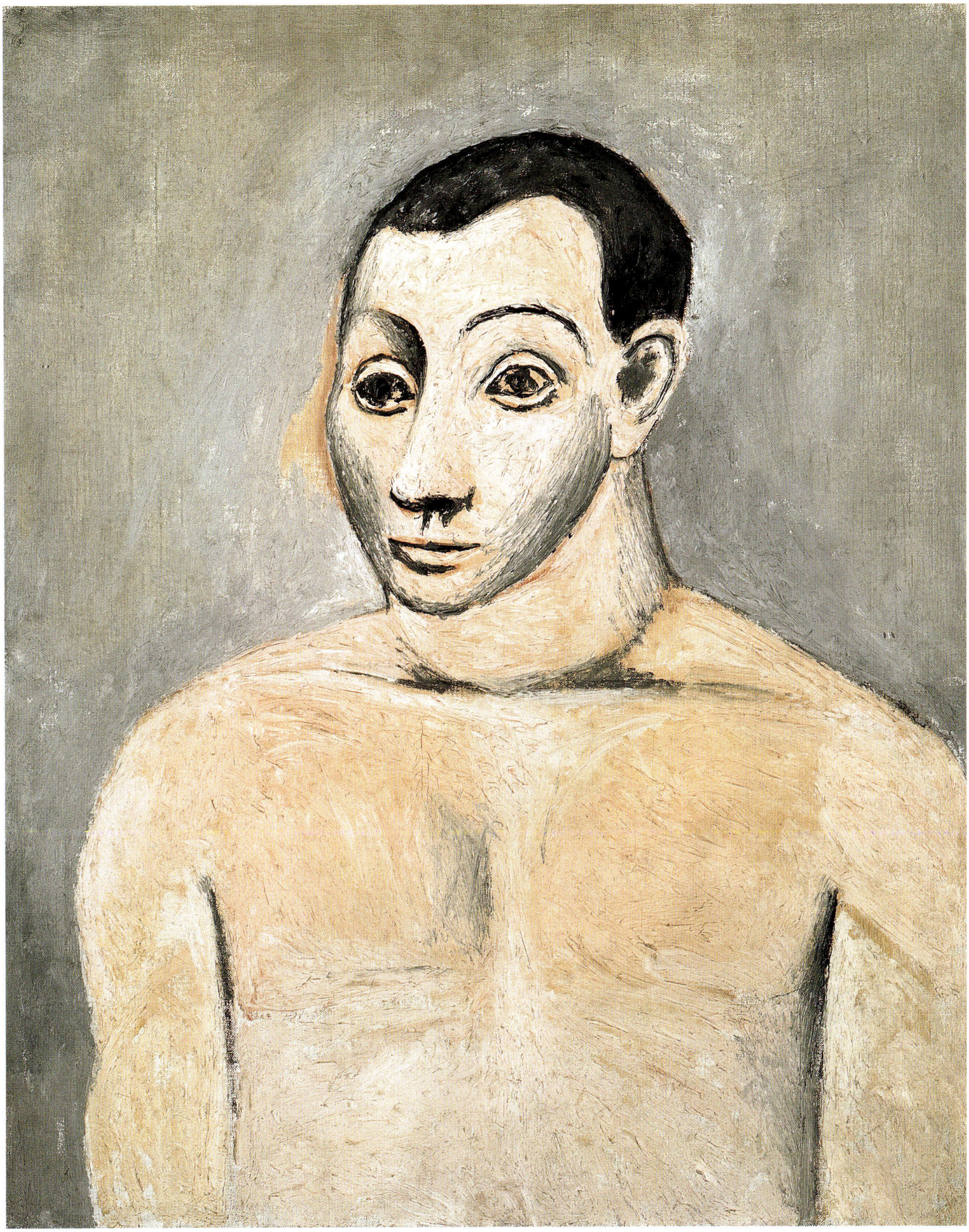

Mother and Child

Summer 1907, Paris
Oil on canvas
81 x 60 cm
MP 19

Everything contributes to making this an outstanding work from this period of Picasso's career – the violence of the contrast between the colours, the exaggerated stylization of the monolithic, mannequin-like faces and bodies, the wild, brutal handling of the child's face... and, finally, the unusual interpretation of the theme of motherhood.

The use of hatchings on the faces and part of the background enables the execution of this canvas to be situated immediately after *Les Demoiselles d'Avignon* (1907, New York, Museum of Modern Art), to which it acts as a postscript, and before his *Nude with Drapery* (1907, St Petersburg, Hermitage Museum), which it heralds. The stripes no longer simply add shading or suggest relief, but serve to integrate the figure into the background, by creating plastic rhythms common to both. Neither can this network of marks be associated with the scarification on African masks, which is always symmetrical, since Picasso used hatchings to emphasize asymmetry. The disproportionate eyes and nose recall the conventions of ancient Iberian sculpture, but are carried to extremes here. The woman's head is taken straight from certain studies of women made for *Les Demoiselles d'Avignon*, particularly in the shape of the chignon, while the expressive force of the huge-eyed child's face, streaked with hatchings, is somewhat evocative of certain African masks. This figure is, moreover, a very strange one, closer to a puppet or an old man than a child. The simplification of forms, the flat zones of colour, the palette, dominated by blue, green and black, and the geometrical framing device in the background testify to the influence of Henri Matisse.

The theme of motherhood appeared at clearly defined moments in Picasso's career: during the Blue and Rose Periods, and then in the 1920s after the birth of his son Paulo. It is therefore surprising to find this theme in 1907, after *Les Demoiselles d'Avignon*, i.e. after iconographic preoccupations of an entirely different kind.

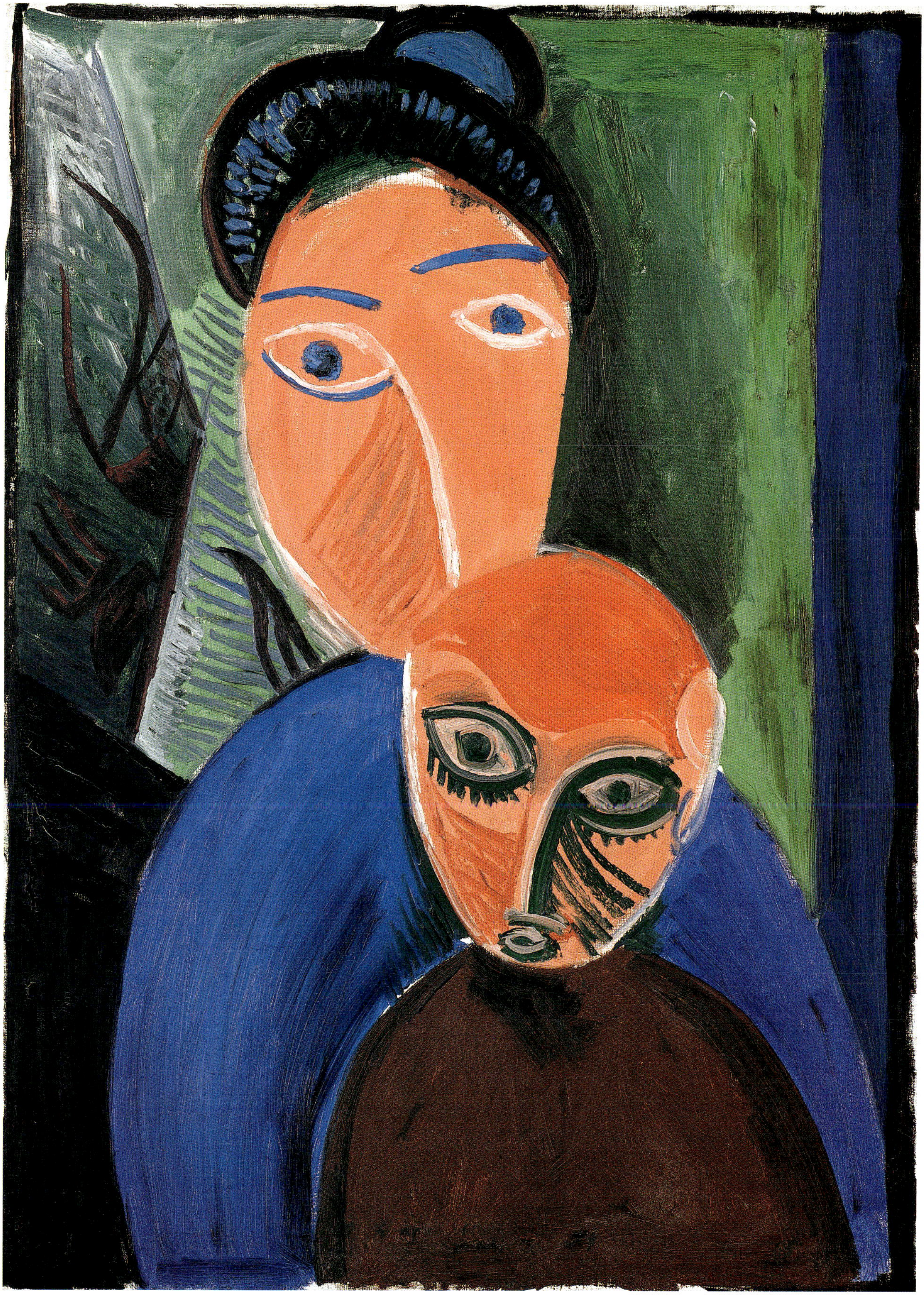

Three Figures under a Tree

Winter 1907-1908, Paris

Oil on canvas

99 x 99 cm

MP 1986-2

Throughout the autumn of 1907 and up until winter 1908, *Les Demoiselles d'Avignon* (1907, New York, Museum of Modern Art) continued to haunt Picasso. The women he painted were extremely stylized, inspired by Negro art. Alone or in groups, they eventually became a series entitled "Bathers in the Forest", to which this painting belongs. They were the synthesis of the artist's investigations into fusing rhythm, colour and form and positioning them in space. From *Nude with Drapery* to *Three Women* and *Friendship*, all these works executed in 1907, now in the Hermitage Museum, St Petersburg, show the evolution from the asymmetry of *Les Demoiselles d'Avignon* to the geometrization of Cézanne.

In this work, Picasso adds rhythm to the forms through his use of schematized contours: two lines to define the head, eyes and nose; two curves for the breasts... He links the figures to each other through a network of hatchings. Although the bodies are fragmented and chopped up, they are inextricably joined together, forming a mass of protuberant volumes.

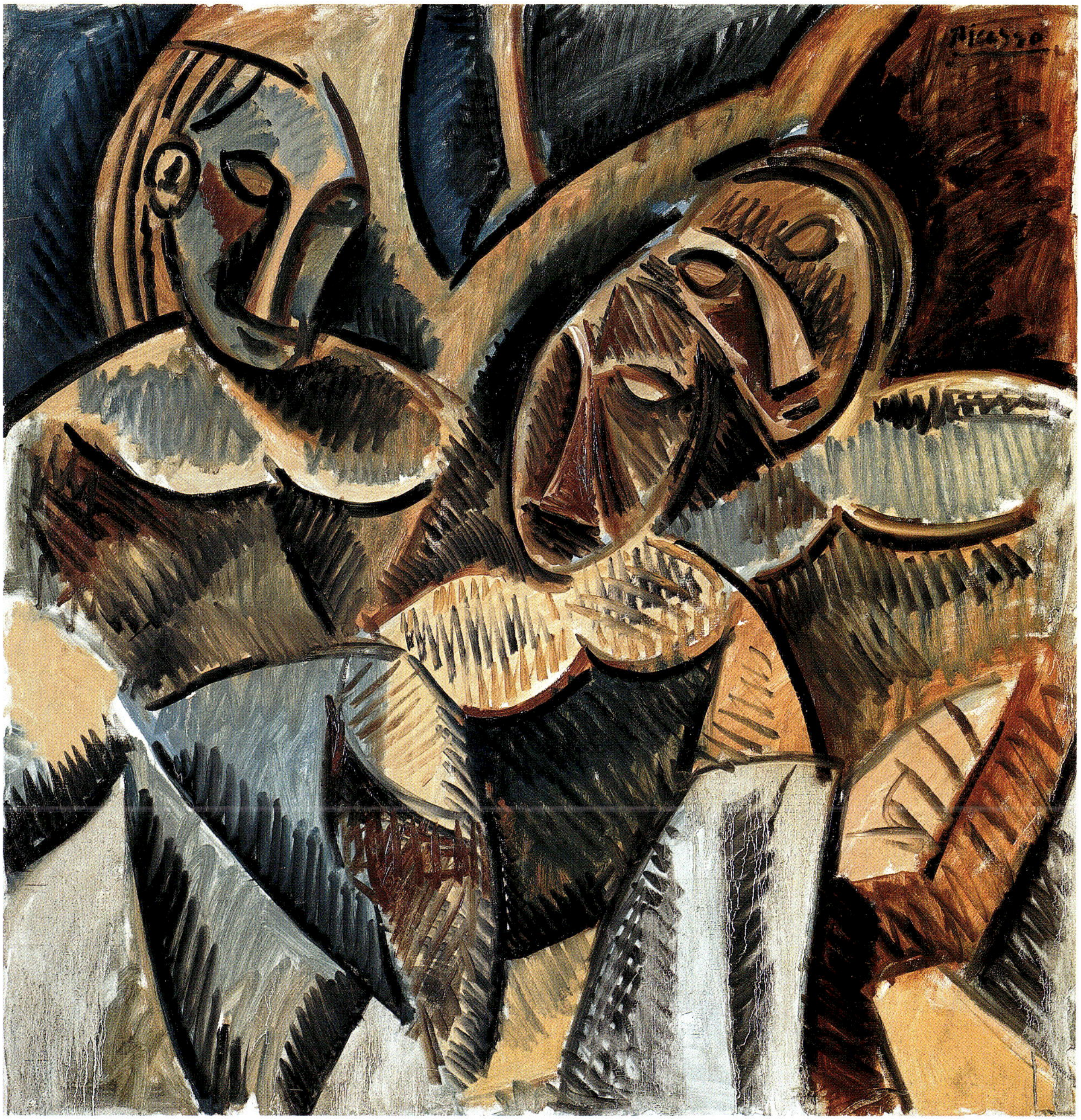
Picasso

Man with a Guitar

Autumn 1911-1913, Paris

Oil on canvas

154 x 77.5 cm

MP 34

The characteristics of Analytic Cubism – monochrome grey, brown and ochre, touches of translucent scumbling, volumes fragmented into facets and geometrized planes – can all be found in this painting. Picasso began *Man with a Guitar* in 1911-1912, and then reworked it in 1913, as is indicated, on the one hand, by the inscriptions on the back of the canvas and, on the other hand, by the various, clearly distinct stages of its execution. This work is a perfect example of Cubism's evolution between 1911 and 1913, from the figuration of volume in broken facets, the dissection of the homogeneous form and its integration into the spatial framework to the introduction of block capitals (here the letters KOU) and realistic details (the volute of the chair, the glass), which act as reference points. This painting, together with *Man with a Mandolin* (Paris, Musée Picasso), belongs to a series of eight large-scale compositions, executed in 1911-1912, representing male or female figures with musical instruments. But these two works are exceptional in that they are full-length portraits: Picasso was thus obliged to enlarge them by adding a strip of canvas at the bottom, which confers an "unfinished" aspect upon them, or at the very least sets them apart from the rest of the series.

The singularity of *Man with a Guitar* stems mainly from the way in which it is divided up into three distinct, superimposed parts, differentiated by their colours and pictorial vocabulary, which correspond to well-defined phases in Cubism. The upper part of the canvas, dominated by brown ochre, represents the stage of volumes fragmented into facets; but Picasso subsequently repainted the background so that the contour of the form remained closed. The central part, painted in beiges with luminous, transparent scumbling, is built up in geometric planes around a centre represented by the guitar's sound hole. This instrument, dissected and broken up into several elements, fuses into the flat picture surface. The lighter, more simplified, lower section, which was added on to the canvas, seems to introduce a new pictorial language based on the synthesis of the forms of the object, combined with rectilinear planes and linear construction.

The unity of the painting depends on this notion of gradation, of the diminution of the figure from top to bottom, this progressive movement from heaviness and fullness to lightness and transparency. The conflict between the real object and the background, the flat picture space, is acuter than ever.

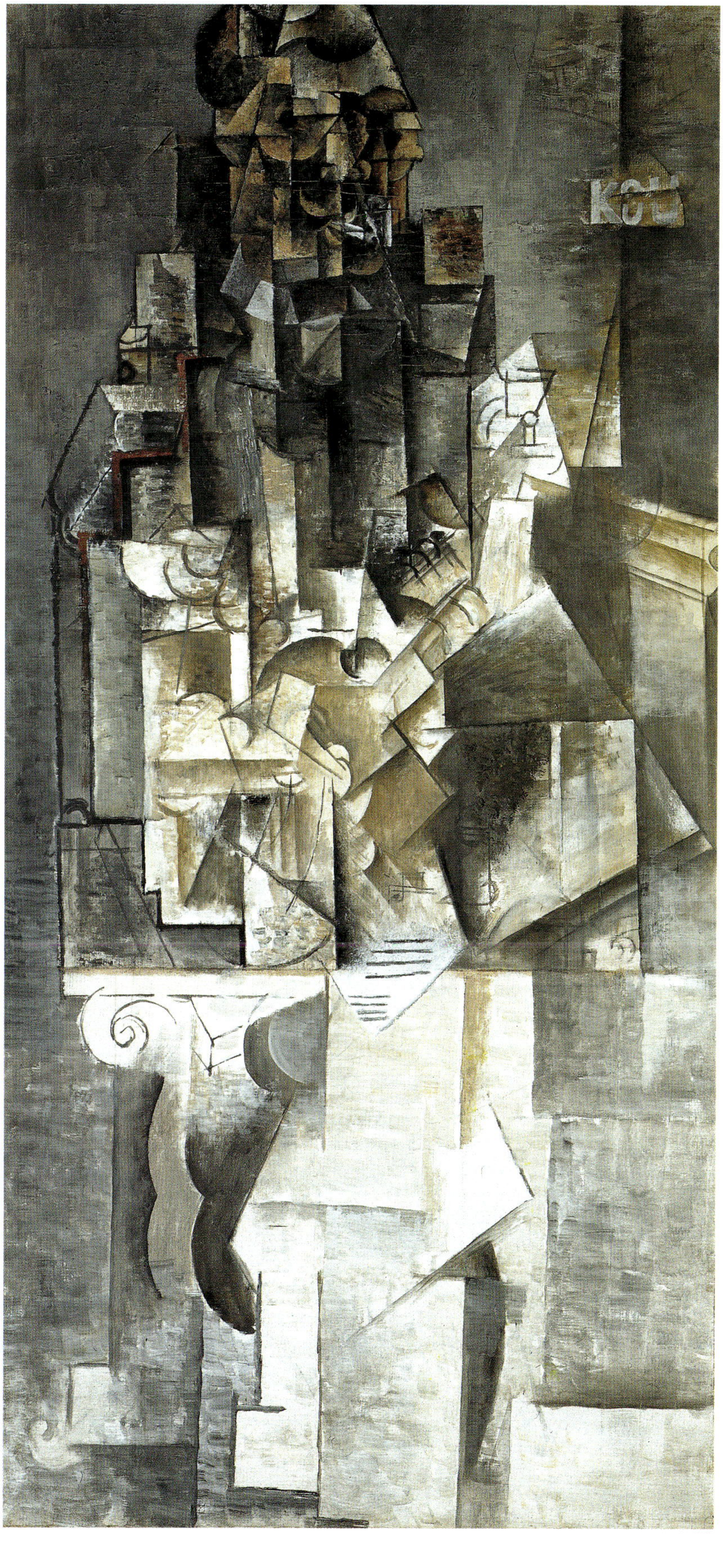
KOU

Still Life with Chair Caning

Spring 1912, Paris

Oil on oilcloth, rope border

29 x 37 cm

MP 36

Still Life with Chair Caning is one of those pivotal, quasi-mythical works, around which revolves not only the history of Cubism but that of all 20th-century art. It was thus not purely accidental if Picasso never let it leave his collection. In early 1912, by using a piece of oilcloth to represent a chair in a picture, Picasso revolutionized the act of painting and called centuries of pictorial tradition into question: why bother depicting an "imitation" – i.e. by using illusionistic brushwork – of something that can "actually" be shown by incorporating a real object? The question of the conflict between art and reality, between the artistic process and the mechanical process is therefore clearly raised. However, ambiguity has by no means been removed, since the oilcloth is not a genuine piece of chair caning, but only a *trompe-l'oeil* of caning. It is thus at once a *mise-en-scène* and a means of challenging a manner of representation.

In the painted part of the picture, the already codified symbols can be recognized – the lemon slice, glass, pipe, knife, scallop shell and the stencilled capital letters JOU (standing for *journal* [newspaper] or *jouer* [to play]), the usual repertoire of Cubist still lifes dating to this period, an inventory of everyday objects found on bistrot tables.

The oval format, then frequently used to recentre the composition and to avoid orthogonal vanishing points in the corners, is enhanced here by an imitation frame in real rope, which recalls the edge of the table while transforming the picture into an object.

The invention of collage was born out of Georges Braque and Picasso's need to return to reality, when they realized the logic behind Analytic Cubism was leading them towards increasing abstrusity. The introduction of a found object into a work of art paved the way for "ready-mades", assemblage art and Dada and Surrealist collages.

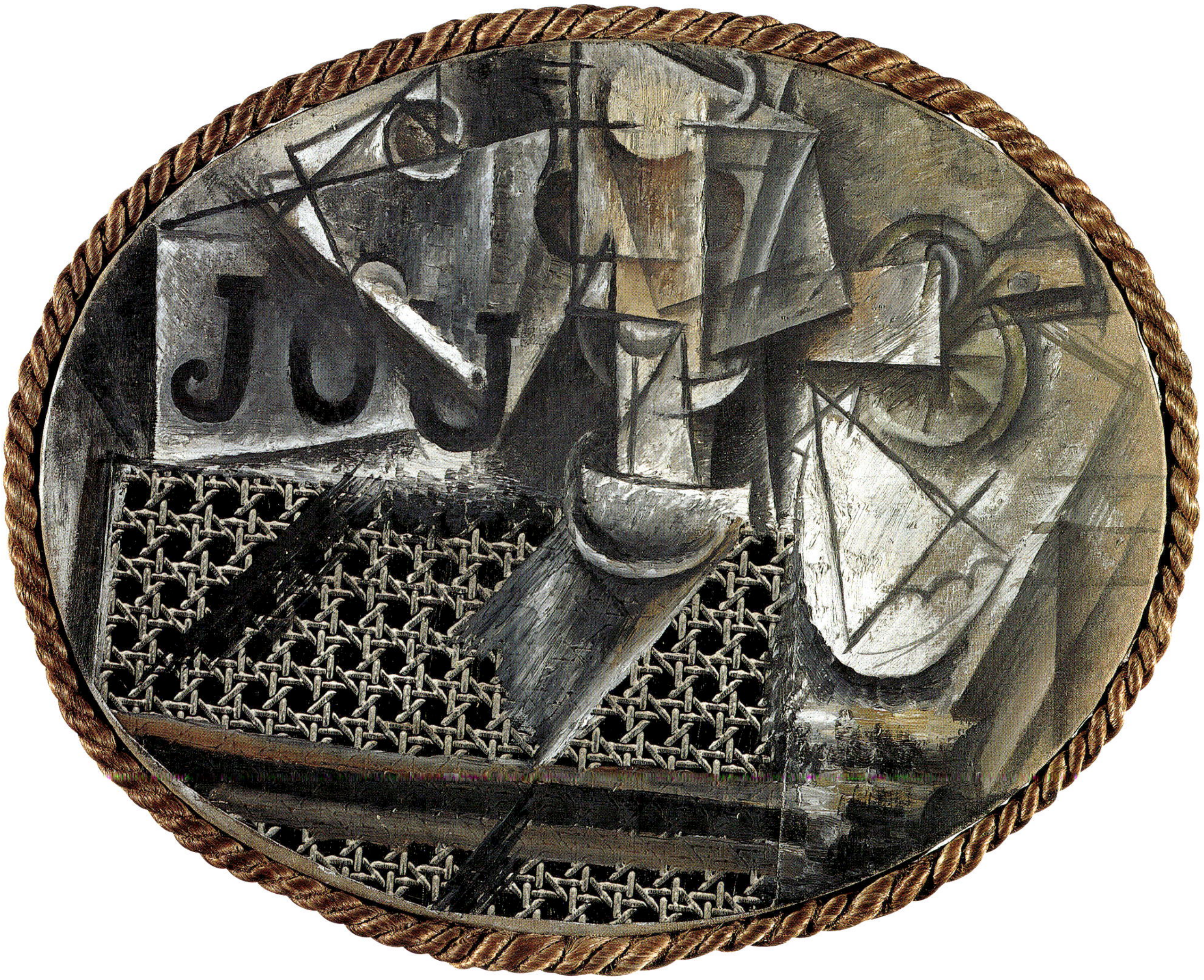
JOU

Violin

1915, Paris
Construction; cut, folded and painted sheet metal, wire
102 x 63.7 x 18 cm
MP 255

The fruit of Picasso's exploration of *papiers collés* (glued papers), i.e. compositions made out of superimposed coloured planes, *Violin* (1915) was the culmination of Synthetic Cubist works in relief, or, in other words, the epitome of an object reduced to rectilinear, geometric planes that seek to convey the instrument's formal structure and abstract architecture rather than its anecdotal peculiarities. The violin can be identified from the two long, brown, hollow rectangles representing its sound holes.

This type of sculpture with openwork, cut-out forms and inverted volumes was inaugurated in 1912 with the famous *Guitar* (New York, Museum of Modern Art), executed first in cardboard, then in sheet metal. This technique of folding both cardboard and metal was an original characteristic of Picasso's work. The folded planes of the sheet of metal he used here incorporated real space to suggest relief. These sculptures that broke away from the closed volumes of in-the-round statuary paved the way for Constructivism. Yet they differed from their Russian counterparts in that they still needed to be hung on a wall, to be viewed from the front, and hence were pictorial, and in that, by being covered in paint, they rejected the specificity of the medium.

Picasso executed other painted sheet-metal sculptures, such as *Bottle of Bass, Glass and Newspaper* (1914) and *Guitar* (1924), both in the Musée Picasso, Paris, made out of a single sheet of metal, which he likewise cut out and folded.

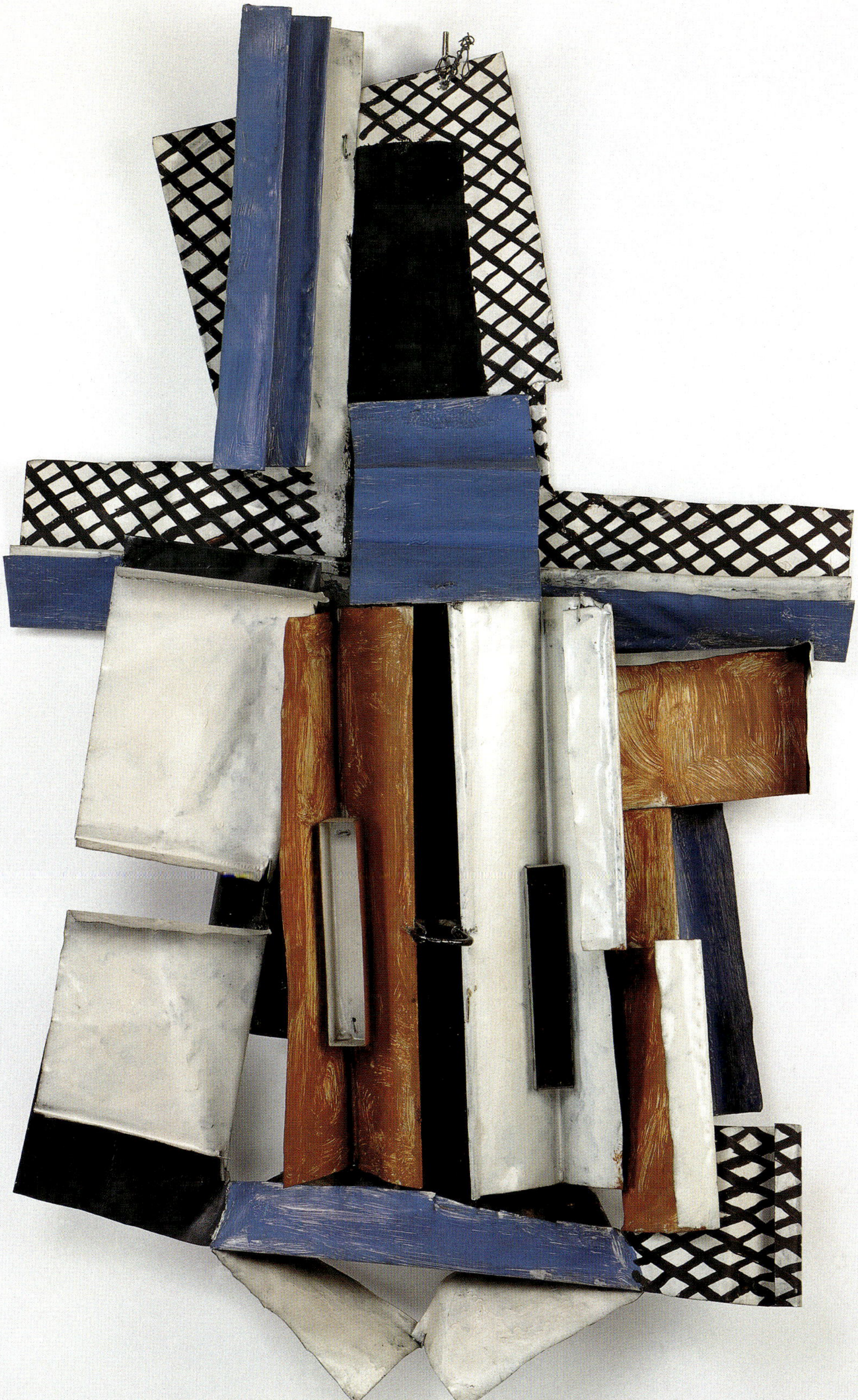

Portrait of Olga in an Armchair

Spring 1918, Montrouge
Oil on canvas
130 x 88.8 cm
MP 55

In 1917, while visiting Italy with Jean Cocteau to finalize the stage sets for *Parade*, Pablo Picasso met Olga Kokhlova, a dancer with the Ballets Russes, whom he married in 1918. This picture is one of the first portraits the artist painted of his wife, and, judging from the photograph he used as a model, it is a very faithful likeness. Despite the evident allusion to Ingres' large-scale portraits, there is nothing classical about this painting; Picasso even combines techniques that stem from Cubism with a conventional handling. The deliberately unfinished aspect of the armchair and the rough, hastily sketched marks on the empty, neutral background contrast with the purity of the line and the meticulous details, notably the transparency of the dress, the floral motif, the fan and the jewellery. The figure appears to have been cut out and stuck on a background, from which she is separated by a play of shadows. With its decorative motif, the back of the armchair is treated like a wallpaper collage, and is on the same plane as the figure. Together, they seem to float in space and the young woman does not look as if she is sitting down, for there is no illusion of depth. Picasso has consciously omitted the feet of both the armchair and his model. The superposition of different spaces – flat and illusionistic – is characteristic of the dual spatial register Picasso used in his paintings of this period.

With her finely drawn features, her thin mouth and her refined elegance, Olga's rather insipid beauty is enlivened by the special treatment Picasso subjects it to here.

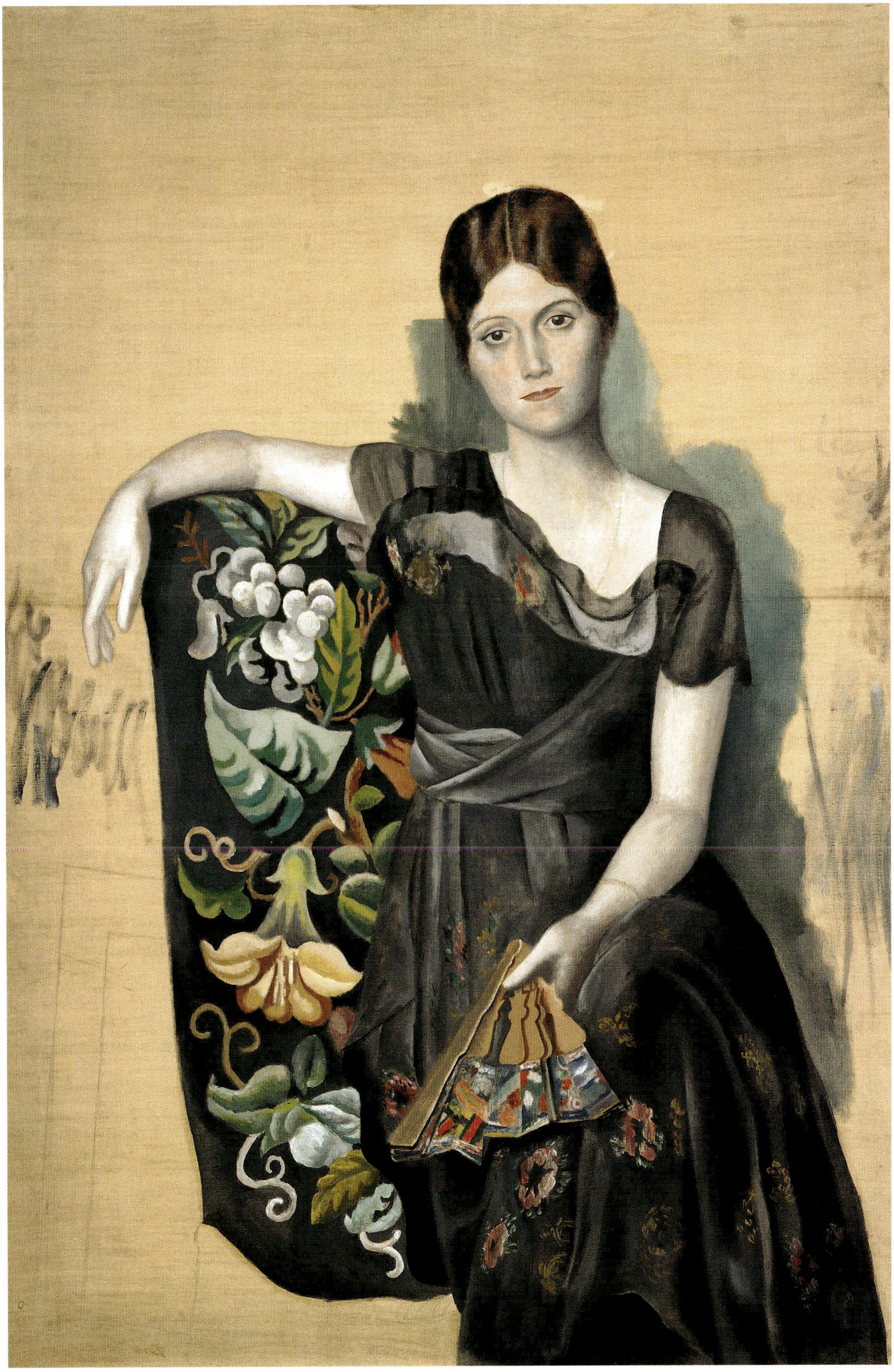

Bathers

Summer 1918, Biarritz
Oil on canvas
27 x 22 cm
MP 61

From 1918 onwards, Picasso spent all his summers by the sea, first in Biarritz, then on the Riviera or in Dinard. These visits gave rise to another cycle of works on the "Bathers" theme. This painting was the first in the series, and was executed during the summer of 1918, in Biarritz, where Olga and Pablo were invited to stay by Eugenia Errazuriz after their wedding.[1]

Despite its small format, this monumental-looking painting contains several pictorial references: there are allusions to Georges Seurat's views of Port-en-Bessin, to Italian Mannerism, to Henri Rousseau's primitivism, and, lastly, to André Derain's "Gothic" style. But the most obvious influence is, of course, that of Jean-Auguste-Dominique Ingres, especially his *Turkish Bath*.

This work, which Picasso kept as a reference, stands apart from the rest of his oeuvre: the slender bodies with tapering limbs, the meticulous realism, the sinuous grace and the direct, primitive treatment are effectively very rare. Picasso's vision of women was usually much more voluminous.

The prosaic nature of these modern-day Venuses in their figure-hugging swimming costumes, the biomorphic forms of the rocks and pebbles, the ecstatic attitude of the standing woman with tentacular hair add a sense of strangeness to this scene, a surreal atmosphere which can also be found in certain seascapes by Yves Tanguy, and in Picasso's series of Dinard *Bathers* (see pp. 46-47), painted in 1928.

1. Chilean-born Eugenia Errazuriz (1860-1952), wife of the painter José Tomas Errazuriz, made friends with Picasso when he worked with the Ballets Russes.

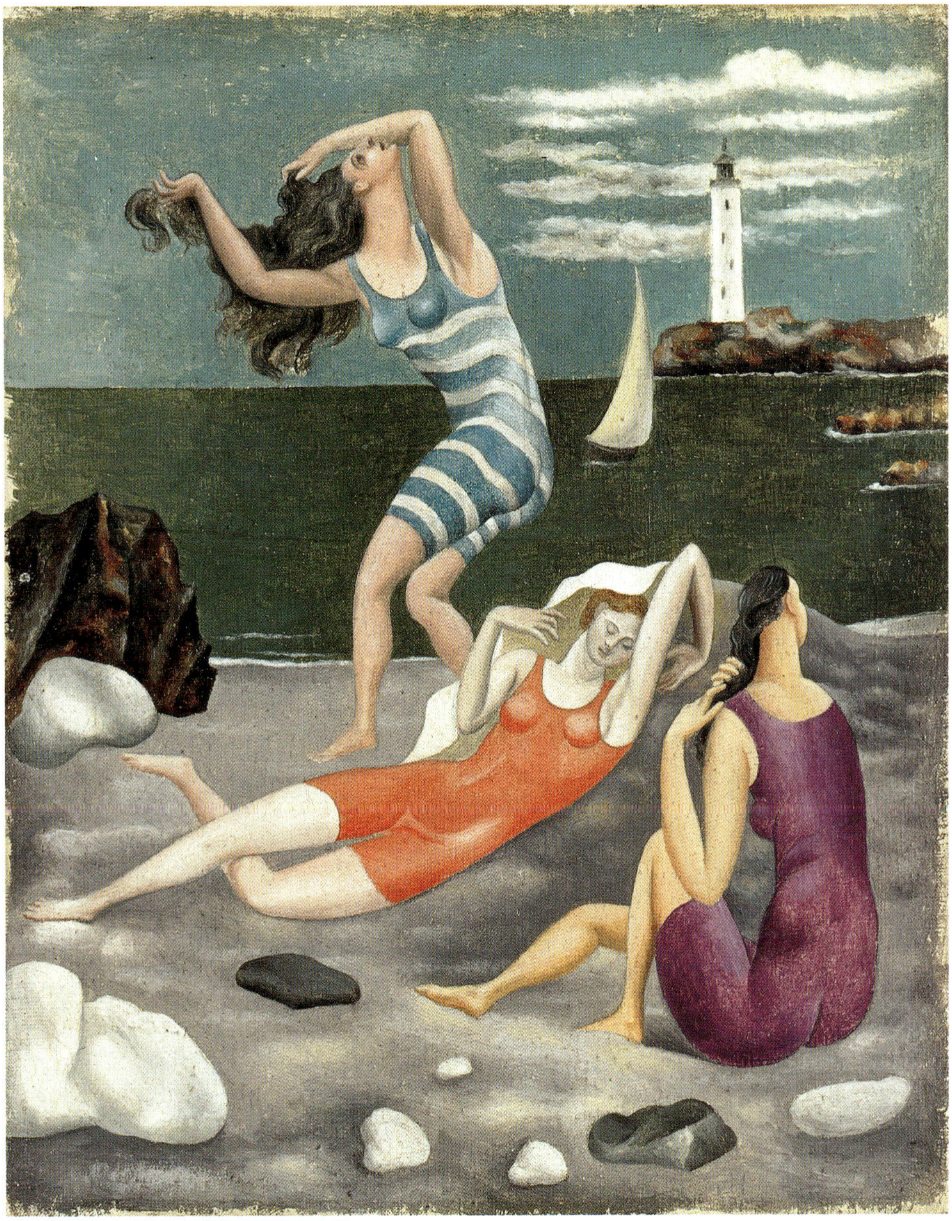

Seated Woman

1920, Paris

Oil on canvas

92 x 65 cm

MP 67

The solid, powerfully modelled, heavy features of this huge-bodied *Seated Woman* testify to Picasso's interest in ancient Roman statuary. In this series of colossal women dating to 1920-1923, one finds the same large, heavy-lidded, expressionless eyes and the nose that looks like an extension of the forehead: "Doe-eyed Junos whose massive square hands clasp stone cloth."[1]

The white draped garment is also a reference to Antiquity, but like the tablecloths in Paul Cézanne's *Still Lifes*, the drapery looks as if it is made out of stone and acquires the same consistency as the body. Picasso gives these giantesses a solidity, a statuesque gravity, and plays on their proportions to emphasize their monumental character. The hands and feet here are out of all proportion with the rest of the body. The very collected pose, enclosing the body in a rectangle balanced on a four-toed foot as broad as a pillar, makes this woman look like a block of stone. The nonchalant gesture made by her fingers recalls the postures of certain figures painted by Ingres. But, in this work, sensuality makes way for deep reverie and a fixed, expressionless gaze.

The "Seated Woman" or "Woman in an Armchair" theme, the first example of which was the pensive, immobile *Barefoot Girl* (1895, Paris, Musée Picasso) – watching and being watched – was one of the artist's favourite motifs. Handled in different ways, it recurred throughout his career.

1. Jean Cocteau, *Picasso*, Paris, Stock, 1923, p. 13.

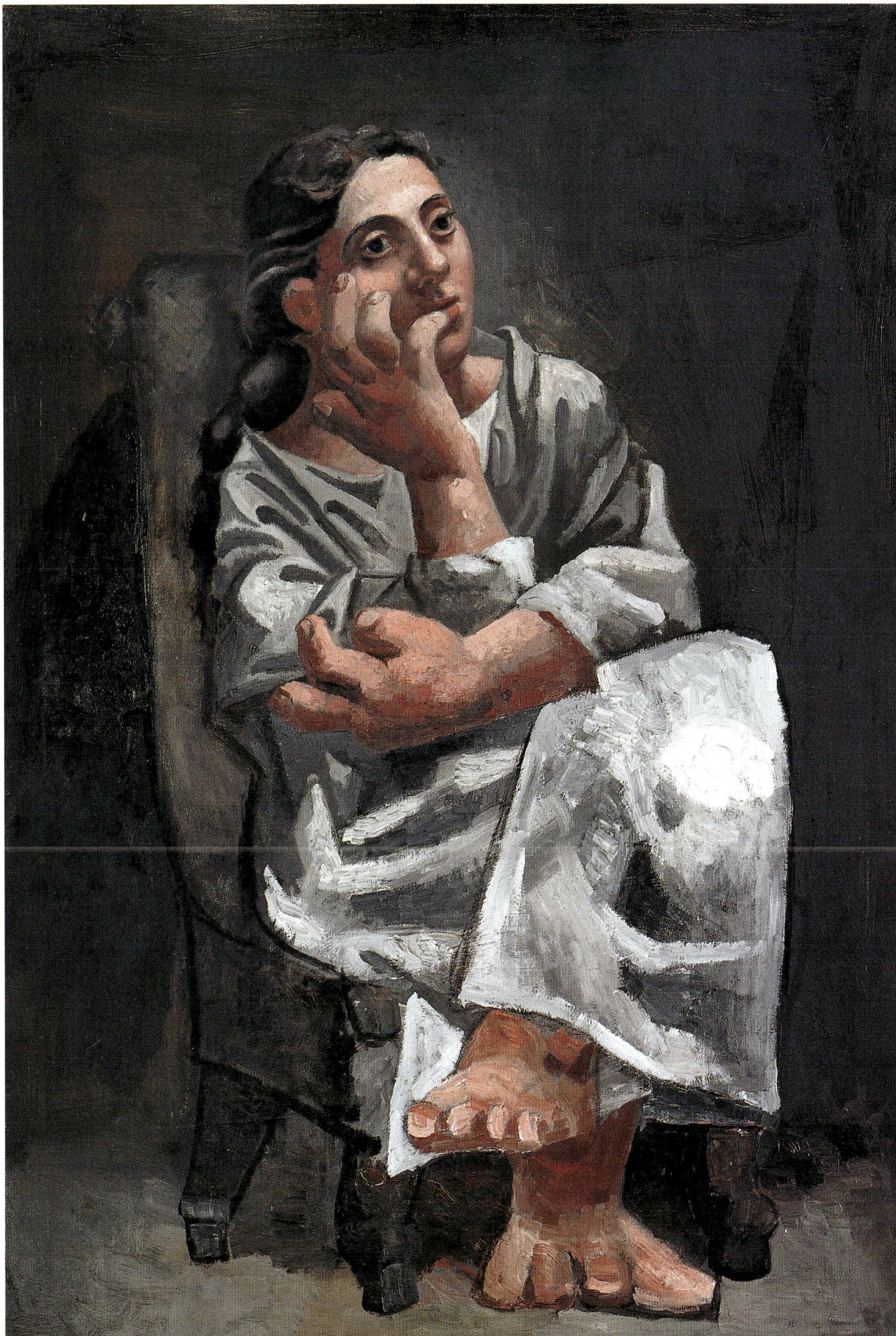

Two Women Running on the Beach (The Race)

Summer 1922, Dinard

Gouache on plywood

32.5 x 41.1 cm

MP 78

The visual impact of this frenetic work is due to the contrast between the heaviness of these marmorean giantesses and the lightness of their movements; swept along by the speed of their running, they seem to be on the verge of flying into the air, despite the weight of their massive legs. The wider the gap between two contradictory images, the stronger the tension: the energy that propels two bodies into space. Picasso used various formal devices to suggest this dynamism: the floating hair and garments; the woman with her head thrown back recalls the goddess Thetis' pose in Jean-Auguste-Dominique Ingres' *Thetis imploring Jupiter* and those of the *Bathers* in the 1918 series (see pp. 28-29); the other woman's face turned to one side; the robustness of the bodies and, above all, the powerful use of diagonals and horizontals to structure the composition. The idea of ascension is in fact expressed by the triangle formed by the two diagonals of the uplifted arms, while the large arm, thrust forward and held in the prolongation of the extended leg behind, creates an impression of the woman being inordinately outstretched and indicates speed.

These figures were inspired by bathers dancing on the beach and studies of dancers made when Picasso worked with the Ballets Russes, but the allusion to Antiquity shown by the drapery urges one to also look to the painted or sculpted maenads of ancient Greece.

Picasso's decision to use an enlarged version of this gouache for the stage curtain for Sergei Diaghilev's ballet *Le Train Bleu* (1912), with music by Darius Milhaud and libretto by Cocteau, was hardly accidental, since the action took place on a fashionable beach and the ballet was a celebration of life in the open air, nudity and sport.

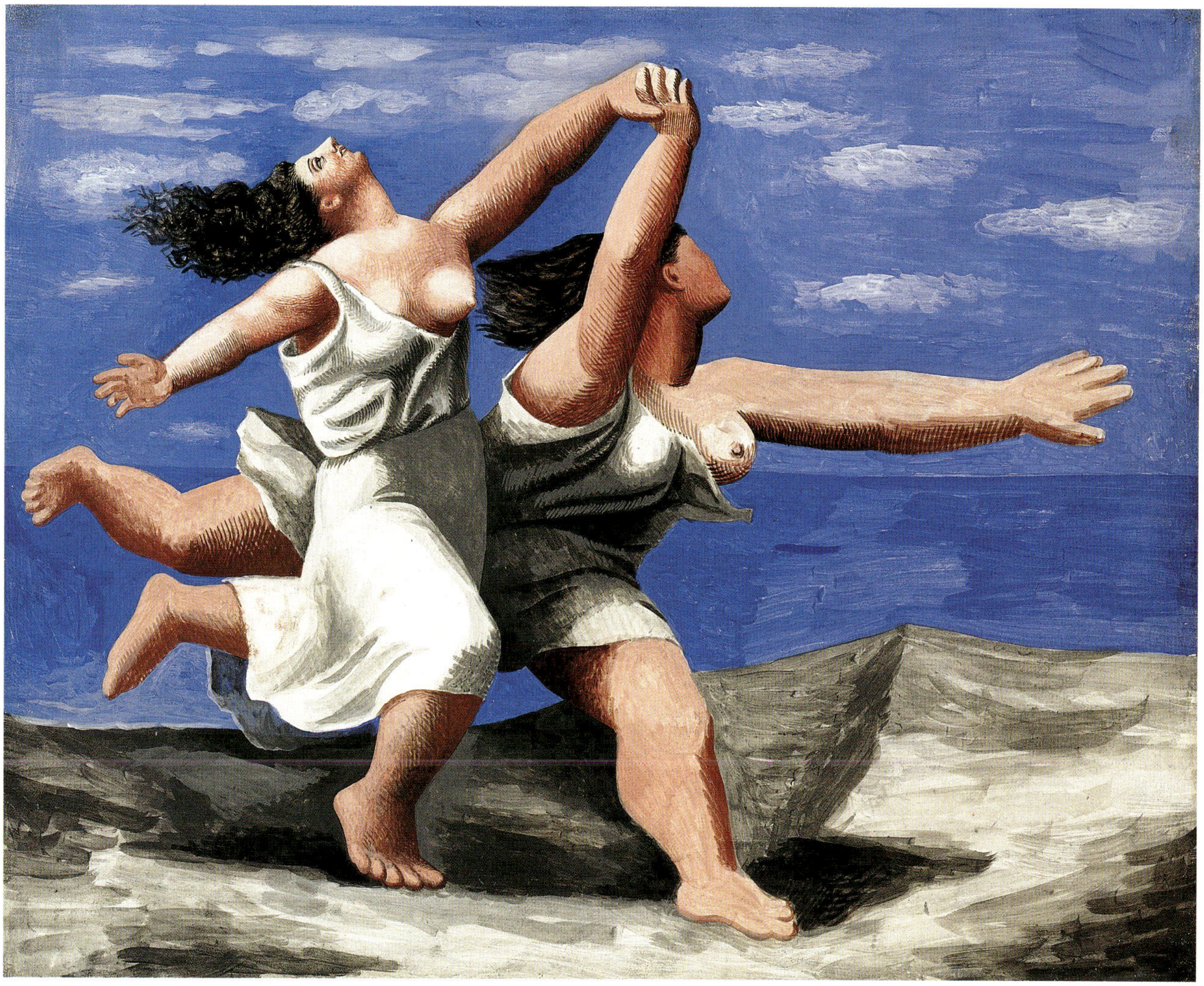

Family at the Seashore

Summer 1922, Dinard

Oil on wood

17.6 x 20.2 cm

MP 80

A monumental work despite its small format, *Family at the Seashore* is a mysterious, poetic painting which may be interpreted as a vision of paternity. These three figures beside the sea no doubt represent Olga Kokhlova, the painter himself and their new-born son, Paulo (b. 1921). It is a triangular image of the family, whose base is the young father's outstretched body and whose summit is the mother's attentive, protective, tilted head.

The woman, in fact, seems to be protecting both the child and the father, who has deliberately depicted himself asleep, in a reserved, modest pose, with his hand covering his genitals.

The symbolic gesture of the child's finger touching the father's ear is reinforced by the mother's arm. All the blood ties have been re-formed and allude to procreation.

This outstanding representation of the family, for which some preparatory studies still exist[1] and which can be linked to *Maternity* (1921, Chicago, Art Institute), is far removed from the conventional, classical images of motherhood that Picasso depicted in this same period, although submission to the triumphant mother, to the nursing mother, is still expressed. The poses of the figures recall the artist's recurrent "Watcher and Sleeper" theme, but in this painting, it is the man who is asleep, watched over by the woman. Because of the references to Antiquity, should one perhaps see this as a portrait of Ulysses washed ashore and found by Nausicaa?

1. Zervos V, 173, 174.

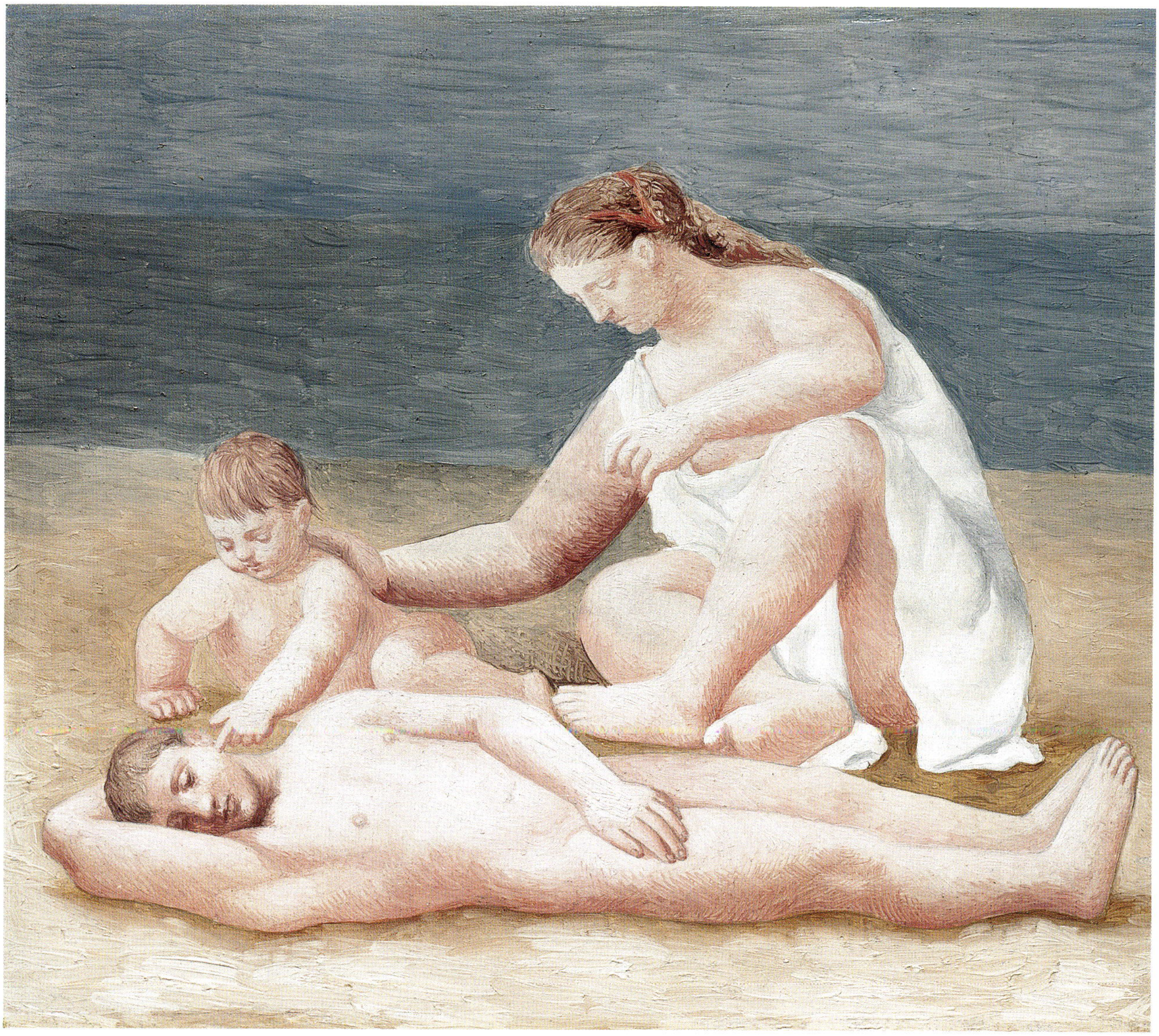

The Pipes of Pan

Summer 1923, Antibes

Oil on canvas

205 x 174 cm

MP 79

Unanimously recognized as a masterpiece of the artist's neoclassical period, this painting, which Picasso no doubt regarded as a pivotal work, never left his studio.

All the critics agree on the simplicity, grandeur and nobility of the composition and its distinctly Mediterranean character: "Through the humanistic tradition, which from Cézanne to Giotto goes back to the pediments of Olympia, Picasso revived the world of rustic nobility and harmonious plenitude that we nostalgically inhabit."[1] This is the work in which Pierre Reverdy sees the application of classicism's golden rule – the subordinaion of the individual parts to the whole. In spite of these reminiscences of the Antique, the atmosphere of the painting is obviously not an evocation of the classical or pastoral idyll. The two young men are powerfully-built fishermen with enormous hands and feet. Ugly swimsuits have replaced the Antique drapery, thereby emphasizing their uncultivated nature. There is no idealization in this work, in which the influence of Paul Cézanne's *Bathers* is evident.

The painting's most perplexing feature is the background made up of cubes and large vertical façades flanking the two horizontal bands that represent the sky and the sea. The space thus created, which evokes the stage-like space, tends to close in around the figures, to suggest depth, and forms a contrast with the modelling of the bodies. The companion piece to this male couple, the symbol of friendship, can be found in *Reading the Letter*, painted in 1921 (Paris, Musée Picasso), and is reminiscent of the adolescents of Gósol (1906).

1. Jean Leymarie, *Picasso, métamorphoses et unité*, Geneva, Skira, 1971, p. 136.

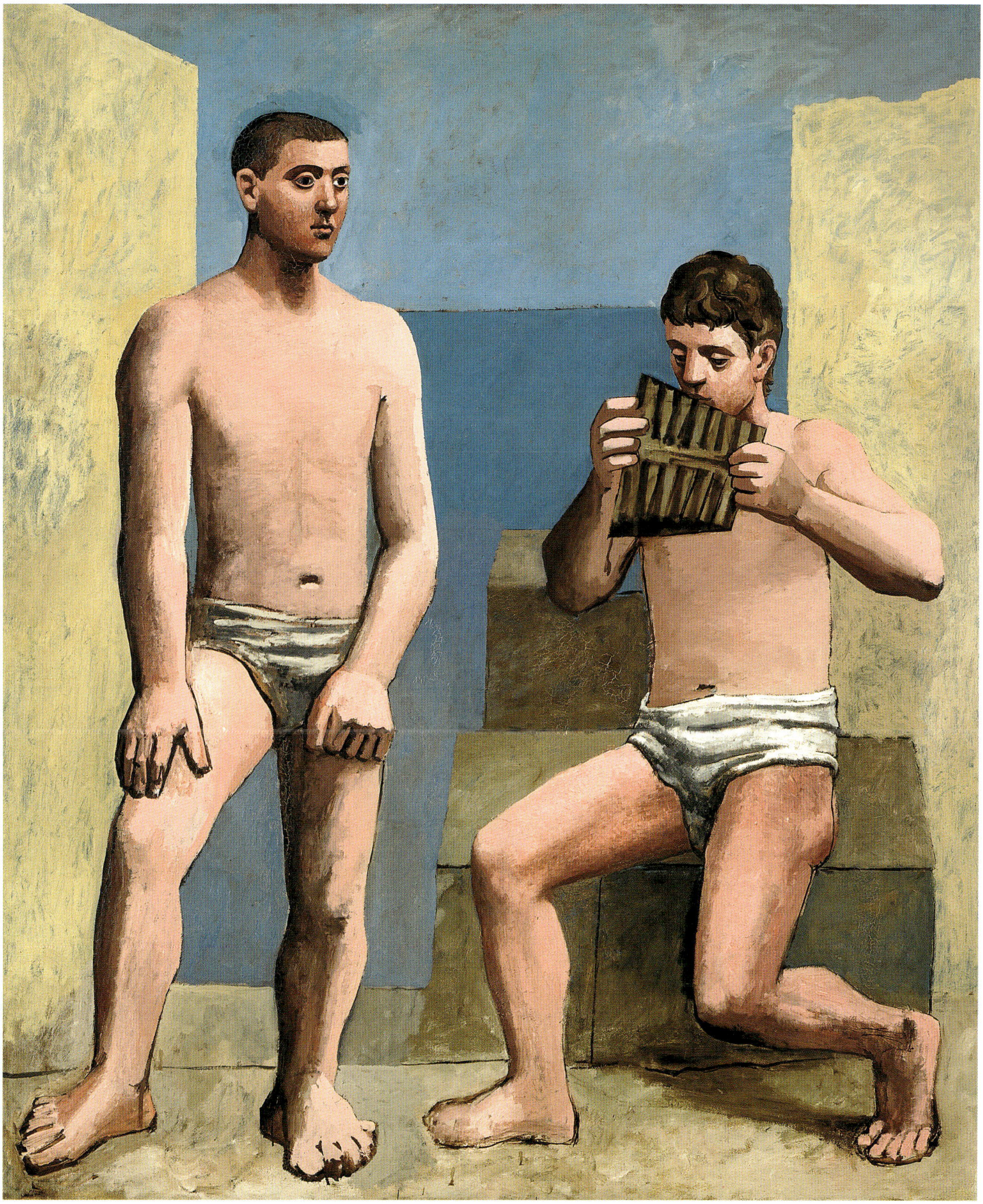

Paulo as Harlequin

1924, Paris
Oil on canvas
130 x 97.5 cm
MP 83

Picasso always showed a liking for the theme of childhood, from *Child with a Dove* (1920, London, Tate Modern), dating from the Blue Period, to *Young Painter* (1972, Paris, Musée Picasso), executed at the end of his life, via numerous representations of his own children – Paulo, Maya, then Claude and Paloma. Like Goya, Reynolds and Renoir, he was one of those painters who was fond of expressing the entire range of emotions evoked by childhood – tenderness, fragility, innocence, reverie and play.

This painting of Paulo aged three is part of a series of several contemporary portraits, two others of which also belong to the Musée Picasso: *Paulo Drawing* (1923) and *Paulo as Pierrot* (1925). Its unfinished quality, revealing a *pentimento*, its neutral, greyish beige background, and the precision and meticulousness of certain details recall the *Portrait of Olga in an Armchair* (see pp. 26-27), the very same chair that can be seen here. Knowing the importance of the Harlequin theme in Picasso's work, it is tempting to interpret the fact that the child is dressed in the famous diamond-patterned costume as the father's idealized identification with his son, especially as the latter gazes at the spectator with the same large dark eyes as the artist. Paulo's fragility and irreality are heightened by the instability of his pose with one leg tucked behind the other. Like Olga in the earlier portrait, he is not really sitting with his elbows resting on the chair, but seems to have been flattened out like a playing card against the dark background of the chair, thereby evoking Édouard Manet's *Fife Player*. Since his feet have not been painted in, he thus floats rather like an apparition on the surface of the canvas, whereas the initial sketch, still visible, showed him resting firmly on his two feet.

With its smooth, porcelain-like finish and finely portrayed features, which demonstrate Picasso's mastery of the classical technique during this period, this portrait belongs to the same tradition as those of the royal children painted by Francisco de Goya.

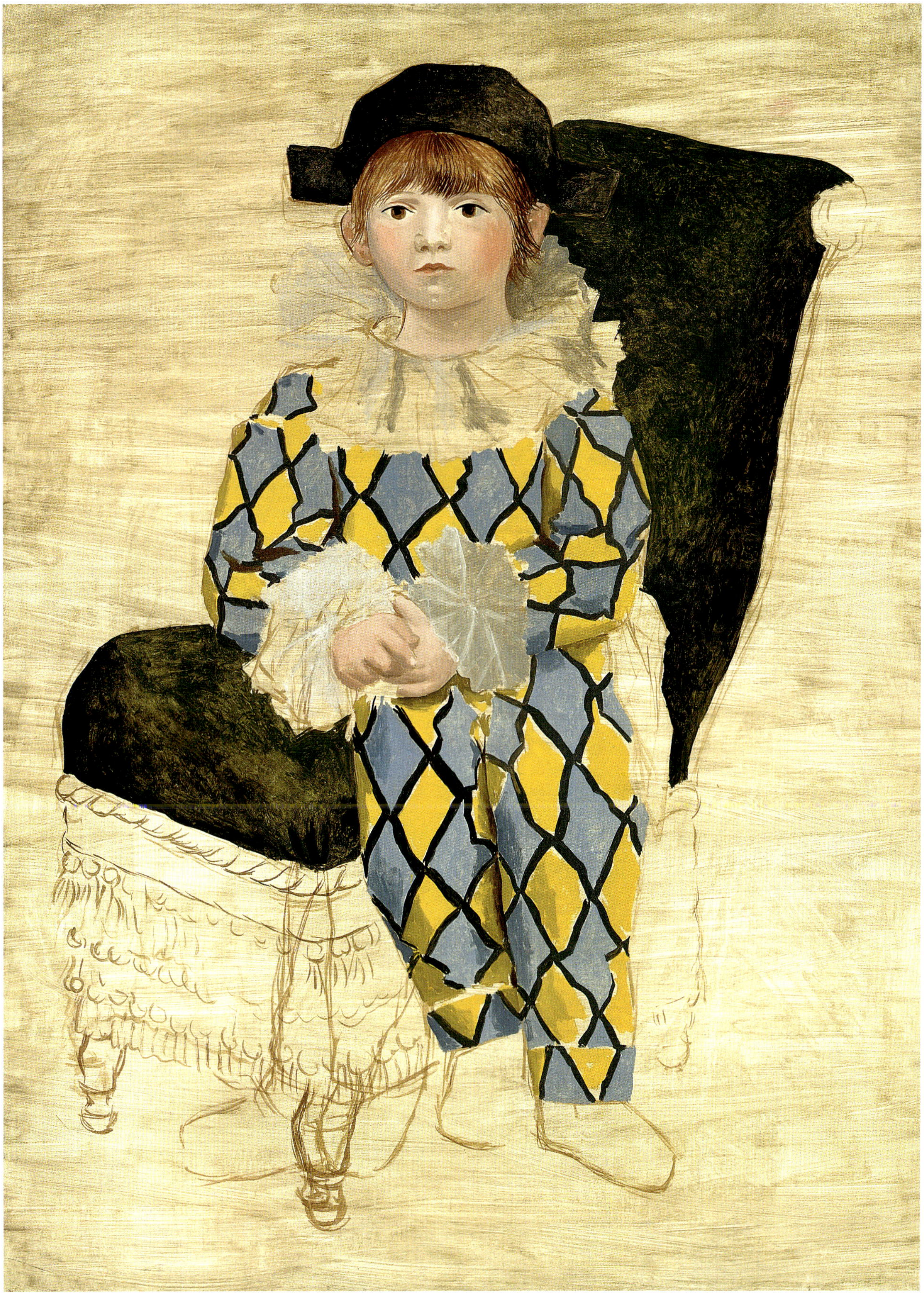

The Kiss

Summer 1925, Juan-les-Pins

Oil on canvas

130 x 97.7 cm

MP 85

The Kiss is an exceptional painting in many respects: an almost unprecedented work, it gave rise to a variety of interpretations. Christian Zervos entitled it *Seated Woman*, while in the catalogue of the Picasso exhibition in Rome, 1953, it was called *On the Beach*. These differences of opinion as to the theme – an interior or exterior scene? – reveal the problems encountered when trying to read the canvas and the perceptual screen that prevented critics from determining the true subject. Nevertheless, in this explosion of colours and forms, how could one fail to recognize a man and a woman locked in a passionate embrace, even if Picasso deliberately complicated its legibility, entwined the bodies and turned sexual organs and limbs upside down, using all the plastic means at his disposal to express erotic rage, sexual frenzy, attraction and repulsion and, above all, the fusion of two beings that takes place in the act of kissing? Equally exceptional in its premonitory style, *The Kiss* is just as important a work as *The Dance* (London, Tate Modern), painted at a slightly earlier date (June 1925). This painting was executed during a visit to Juan-les-Pins with Olga and Paulo, in the summer of 1925; the place and the date are both significant.

The year 1925 was a turning-point in Picasso's career, a time of breaking away, and this work shows the same aggressiveness, makes the same visual impact as *The Dance* – fragmented flat forms, dislocated and loosely reassembled in a puzzle, exaggeration, deformation, overlapping planes and motifs, illusionistic space, Cubist space, and strident, explosive colours are characteristic of both works.

The man's face, with his target-like eye and phallic nose, can be seen on the left; the mouth, at once a female eye and sexual organ, is shared by both faces, which, in addition, seem to be welded together by a band of horizontal lines. The woman's head, seen in profile and from above, is thrown back; the man's left arm is wrapped around her neck, trapping her hair and holding her prisoner. A brown, corrugated cardboard leg with a round white foot can be seen on the left, while the studded sole of a shoe is visible bottom right. The woman's feet have been lifted off the ground, her outspread toes showing either her struggle to resist or pleasure.

This turning-point in the artist's career went hand in hand with the emergence of Surrealism, the watchword being "convulsive beauty" and unrepressed instinct. In Picasso's private life, it also happened to coincide with the first signs of marital tension and conflict with Olga, which would generate a sense of violence and hostility towards women in his painting.

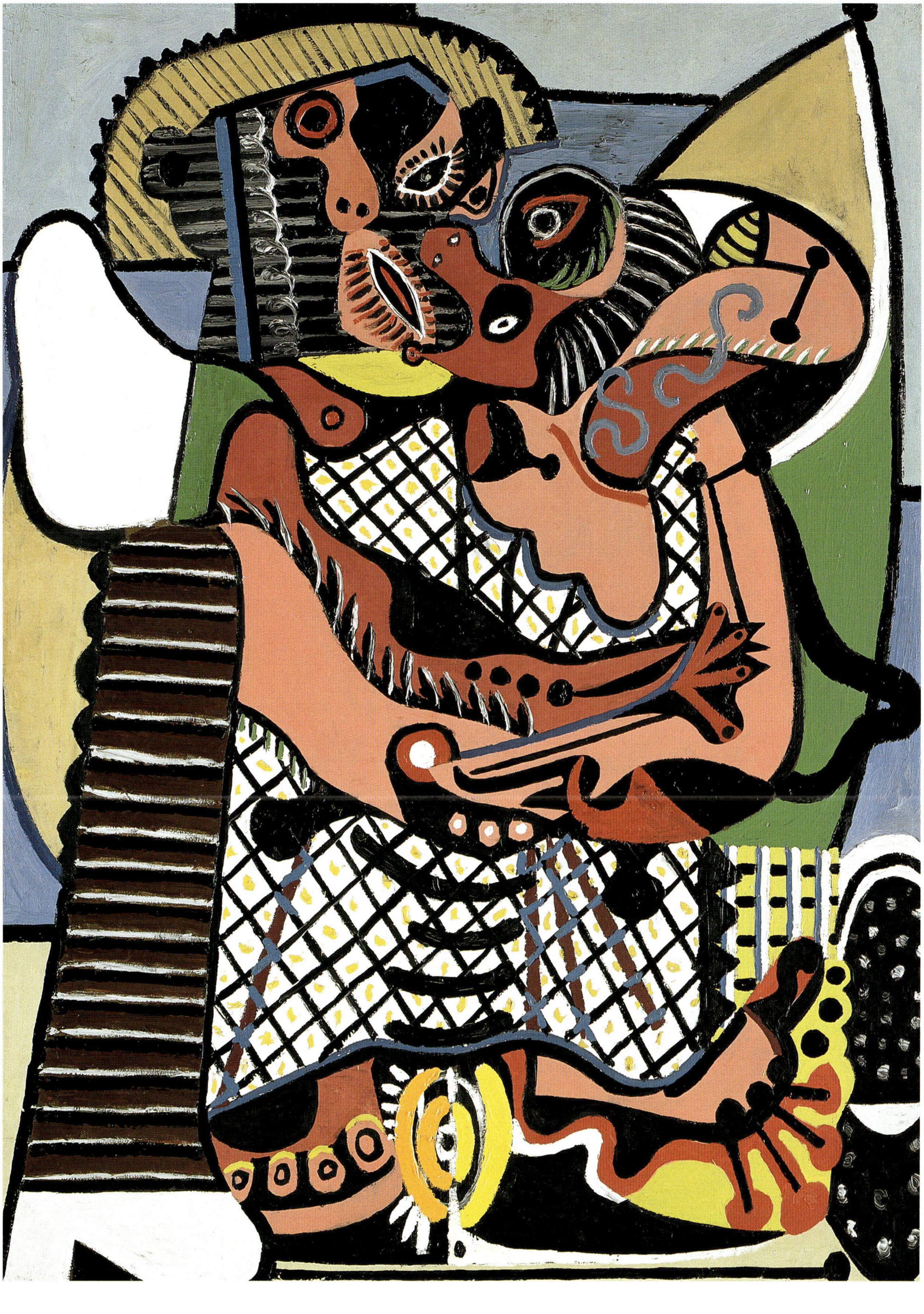

The Painter and his Model

1926, Paris
Oil on canvas
172 x 256 cm
MP 96

This large grey and white canvas was the starting point for infinite stylistic and thematic variations. Contemporary with another large-scale grisaille work, *The Milliner's Workshop* (Paris, Musée National d'Art Moderne), whose combination of curved forms appears as the positive counterpoint to this work, it followed on from curvilinear Cubism and inaugurated a rounded, sinuous style of drawing. As entangled as yarn in a skein of wool, the lines gradually describe the figures. Similar to the Surrealists' automatic writing, in which the brush or pencil was used without rational control to create forms at the prompting of subconscious impulses, this pictorial writing may be related to the drawings and studies Picasso made at this time to illustrate Honoré de Balzac's *Le Chef-d'œuvre inconnu*. The network of interweaving lines defining the two figures here reveals the complexity of the bonds that unite the painter and his model. Picasso makes a direct allusion to the picture Balzac's hero, Frenhofer, endlessly works on, for only a huge foot remains identifiable amidst the inextricable jumble of lines.

The painter and his model was one of the essential themes of Picasso's oeuvre. Confronting man with woman, painter with model, desire with gaze, life with art, was the symbolic figuration of the act of creation.

On the right, the artist can be recognized from his palette; on the left, the woman is reduced to a tiny head, a long neck, different-sized hands and an enormous foot. Visible in the background is a piece of the canvas tacked onto a stretcher and a small picture representing a black and white head.

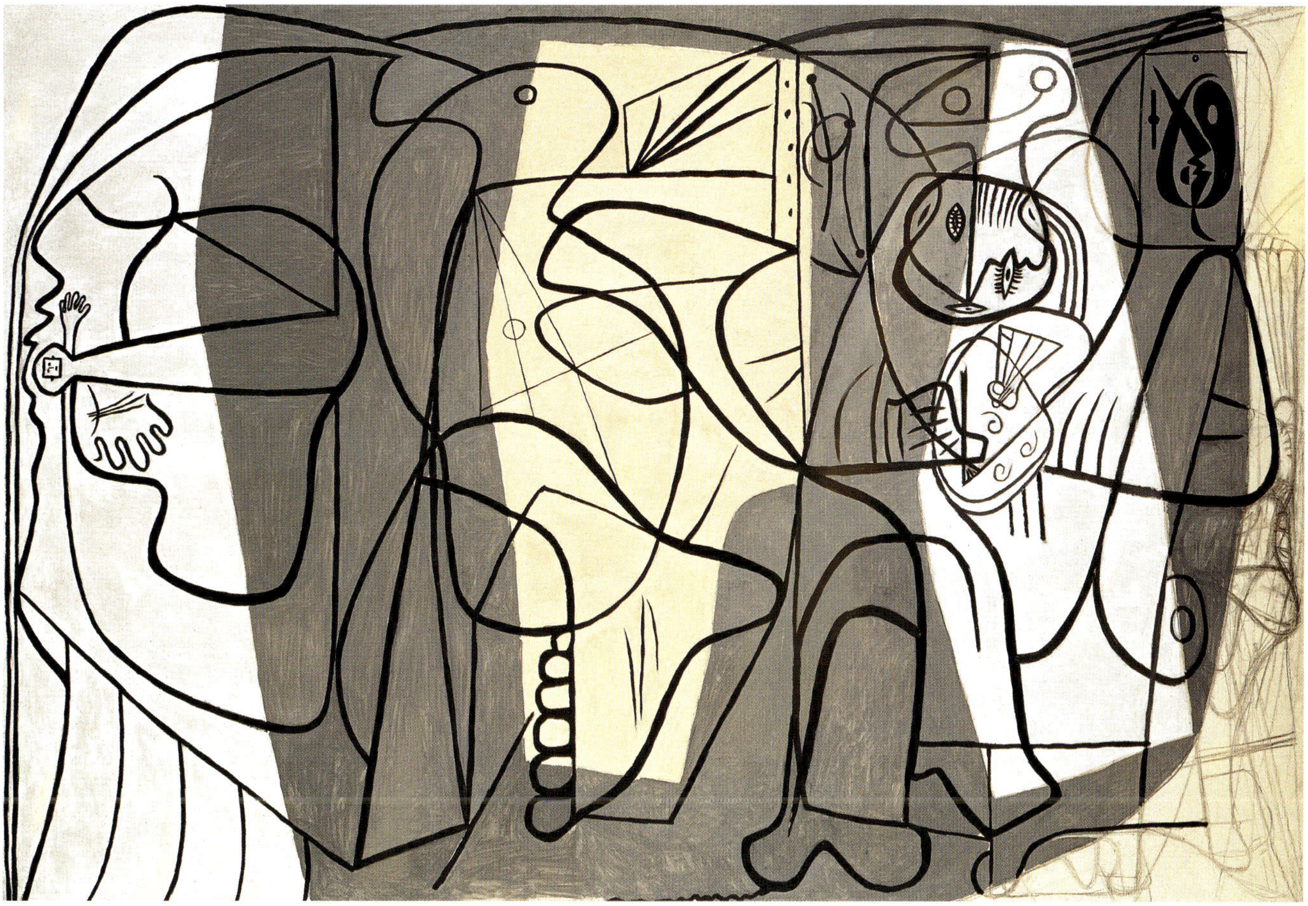

Guitar

1926, Paris
String, newspaper, floor-cloth and nails on painted canvas
130 x 96 cm
MP 87

"Around about the same time, Picasso happened to do something very serious. He took a dirty shirt and sewed it onto a canvas with a needle and thread. And because everything he does turns into a guitar, it was a guitar, for example. He did a collage with nails sticking out of the picture."[1]

Louis Aragon

This canvas is a companion piece to another work depicting a guitar; in one, the nails have been hammered into the support; in the other, they poke out aggressively through the picture. The wretchedness and sordid realism of these dirty, torn rags – one of which has been teased into the shape of a cross, the other bearing a hole in its midst –, the pieces of string that pierce the canvas, the nails and the tears create an impression of unease, pain and strangeness that confers a sense of sacred horror upon these works. In this *Guitar*, Picasso had even thought of inserting razor blades into the corners so that people would cut their fingers when they lifted the work.

The choice of fabric as a medium and the stitching with a needle and thread are characteristics also found in a series of small cardboard guitars dating to the same period, now in the Musée Picasso, Paris. While the composition of this guitar with a newspaper clipping recalls that of the *papiers collés* and Cubist guitars, the pervading spirit and the technique here are very different. It is no longer a collage, but an assemblage, and the discarded materials he has chosen – a scrap of old shirt, a floorcloth – are employed crudely here, more for their power of suggestiveness than for their formal specificity. The Surrealists responded to the work's dramatic impact by publishing a reproduction of it in *La Révolution surréaliste*. The use of nails is reminiscent of certain fetishes bristling with nails in African art, or of witchcraft, when a spell is cast upon a person by sticking needles or nails into an article belonging to him.

Given his antagonistic marital relationship at the time, this work may be interpreted as an expression of Picasso's murderous feelings towards Olga, who is symbolized here by a commonplace, domestic object, the floorcloth.

1. Louis Aragon, *La Peinture au défi*, Paris, José Corti, 1930.

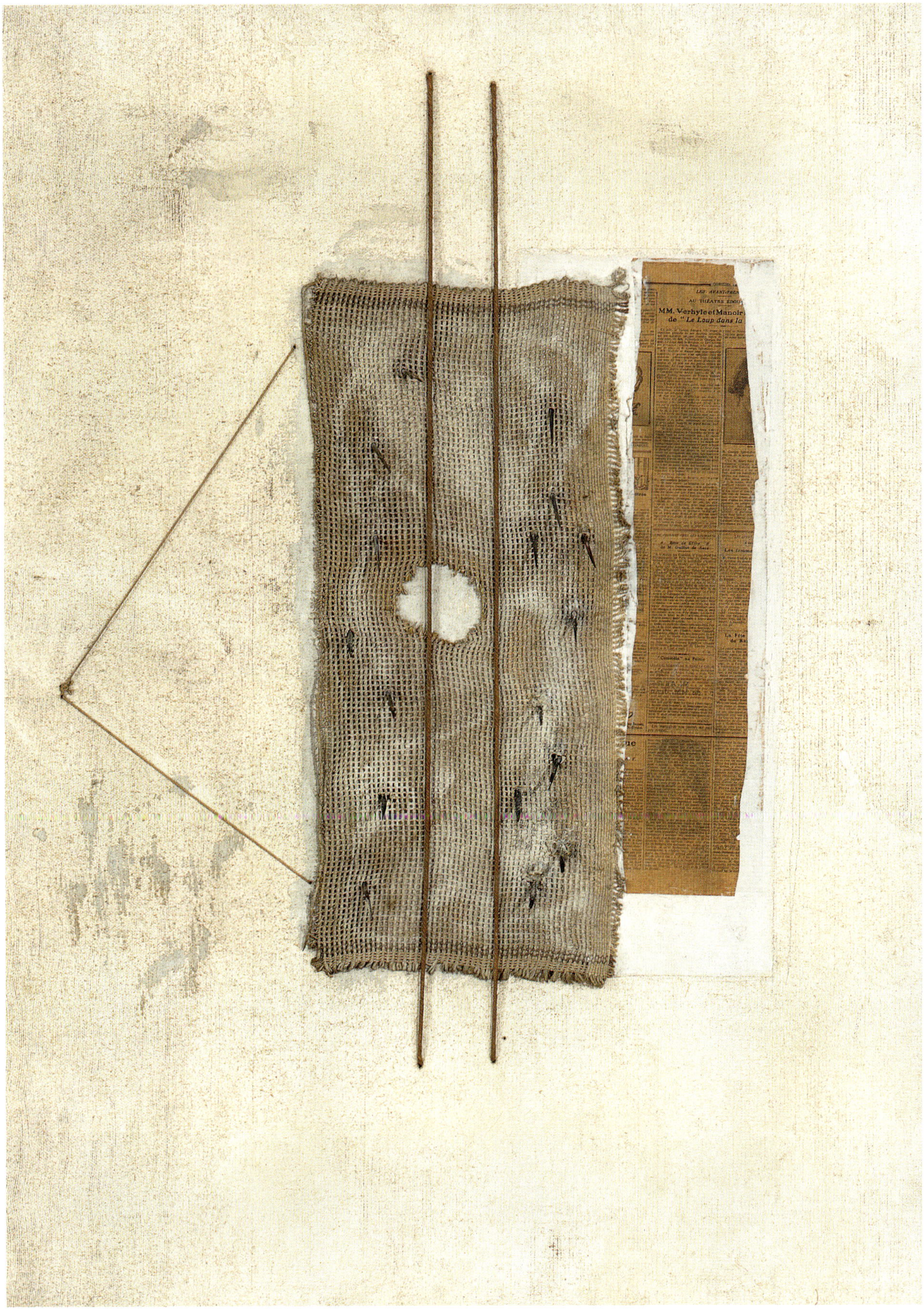
MM. Verhyle et Manoir
de " Le Loup dans la

Bathers

Bather
6 August 1928, Dinard
Oil on canvas
22 x 14 cm
MP 106

Bather opening a Beach Hut
9 August 1928, Dinard
Oil on canvas
32.8 x 22 cm
MP 107

Ball Players on the Beach
15 August 1928, Dinard
Oil on canvas
24 x 34.9 cm
MP 109

"I like keys a lot... it seems very important to have some. It's true that keys have often haunted me. In the series of male and female bathers, there's always a door that they are trying to open with a large key."[1]

Pablo Picasso

Picasso spent two summers in Dinard, in 1928 and 1929, during which he painted the famous series of small canvases on the theme of female bathers. Whether they were based on the prosaic beach hut theme, which first appeared in Picasso's sketchbook in Cannes, 1927, and which he pursued until 1938, or were explorations of the metamorphosis of the female anatomy, the combination of familiar and monstrous elements, humour and mystery, and the latent eroticism in these little beach scenes were well and truly in the Surrealist vein.

The beach hut, at once a childhood memory of the beaches at La Coruña and a real motif seen at seaside resorts, is a symbol that invites a variety of interpretations. Treated as a permanent partner of these female bathers, with whom it is always associated, or confronted, it is a metaphorical representation of Picasso himself, i.e. the concrete image of the body viewed as a home, of the inner life, of the place of refuge constantly threatened by interiority, and beyond that, of the place of mystery. The key is thus not simply a sexual symbol, but rather the key of Revelation, of access to the hidden meaning, to the invisible world. As always in Picasso's work, the little scenes are doubly significant: the starting point is the representation of reality, of everyday life, i.e. the living spectacle before his eyes, as evidenced in the painting of a female bather with a beach ball inspired by a photograph of Marie-Thérèse Walter, or those depicting the frenetic movements of people playing ball in striped swimsuits. But at the same time, these are also "magical pictures",[2] mystical musings that bring into play his secret relationship with the woman and the danger she represents. The beach hut is occasionally transformed into a temple, or a tomb, while sometimes it is the human body itself that assumes the form of the beach hut (*Large Bather*, 1929, Paris, Musée Picasso).

The transparent light of the Breton beaches, the pale tones, the thick use of paint and lively brushwork in relief emphasize both the vehement lyricism of this series and its joyful, poetic atmosphere.

1. Antonina Vallentin, *Pablo Picasso*, Paris, Albin Michel, 1957, p. 90.
2. Christian Zervos, "Picasso à Dinard", in *Cahiers d'art*, no. 1, 1929, pp. 5-6.

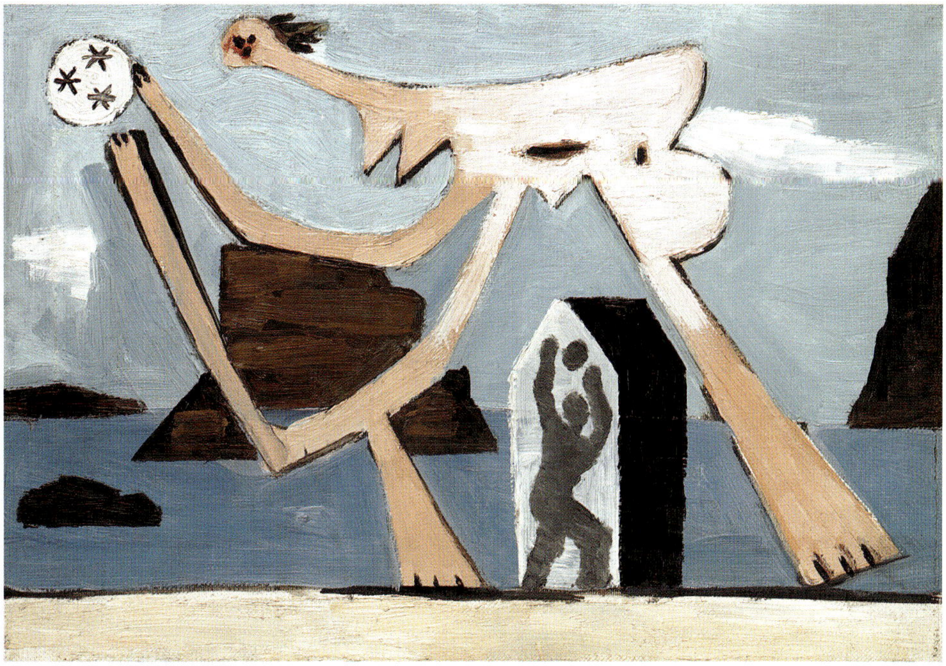

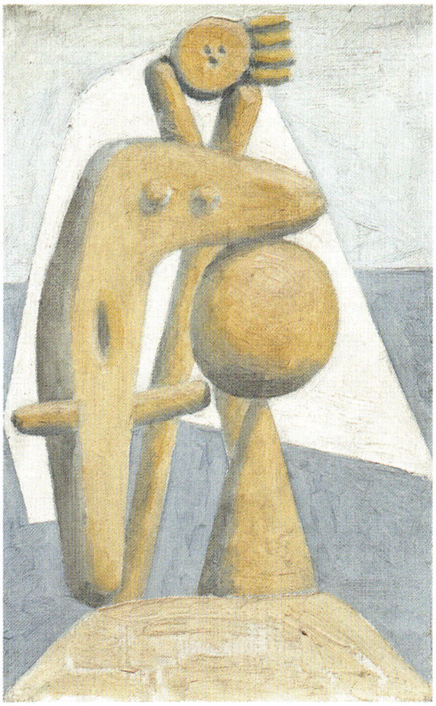

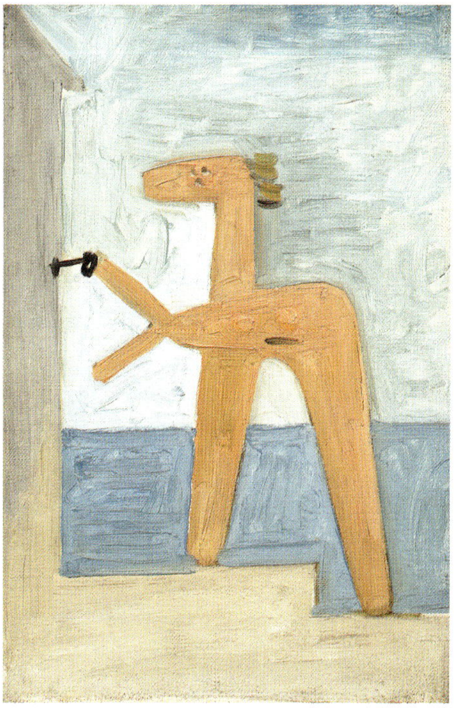

Woman in the Garden

1930-1931, Paris
Painted, welded metal
206 x 117 x 85 cm
MP 267

The size of *Woman in the Garden* makes it one of Picasso's most monumental sculptures. It is an assemblage of iron bars and pieces cut out of sheet metal, and is the fruit of his collaboration with Julio González. The two artists had known each other for a long time, but from 1928 onwards, Picasso, feeling the need to return to sculpture, began to work regularly in González's studio in Montparnasse. The latter put his tools and technical virtuosity in metalwork at Picasso's disposal. No specific drawing is linked to this figure and yet it is easy to spot the motifs that have their equivalent in paintings – the large eucalyptus leaves can be seen in *The Lamp*,[1] a picture dating to 1931; the woman's triangular head with jagged-toothed mouth and hair streaming in the wind appears in the paintings of 1928-1929. The motif shaped like a kidney bean and the circle with a hole in the middle represent parts of the anatomy – belly and genitals. Picasso associates the woman here with plants, thus emphasizing the notion of fertility.

As in his Cubist constructions and metal wire models, Picasso incorporates hollow volumes and empty space into his composition. He then adorns this rigid, abstract, metal structure with realistic, anecdotal motifs, represented by flat, cut-out forms. The combination of two sculptural languages – of lines in space and planes – is characteristic of Picasso's sculpture in the period 1928-1932. The method of assemblage is concealed here by the white paint that adds homogeneity to the work.

1. Zervos VII, 347.

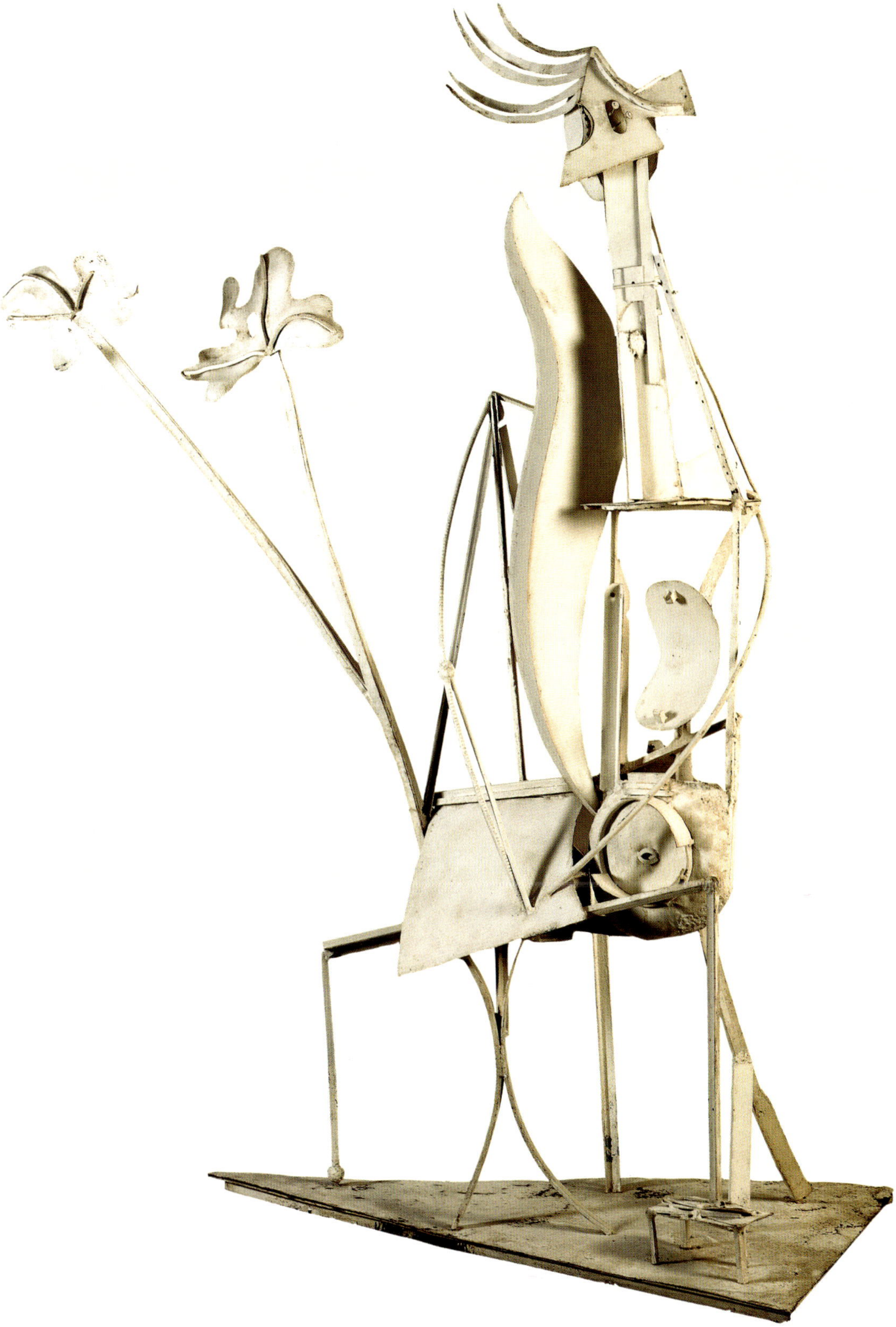

Large Nude in a Red Armchair

1929, Paris
Oil on canvas
195 x 129 cm
MP 113

Picasso did not need to stick razor blades around his canvases to wound the spectator, as he once intended,[1] for the impact of the image alone in some of his paintings, whose cruelty was primarily plastic, could be just as hurtful. *Large Nude in a Red Armchair* is one of those heart-rending works that touch our own inexpressible, interiorized suffering, the only possible concrete image of which is that of bodily collapse and a silent cry of anguish. Everything contributes to expressing this idea here: the flaccid, elongated limbs ending in stumps look like drooping viscera, or tangled-up tentacles thrown onto the armchair;[2] the head has been reduced to a gaping mouthful of teeth, to a pincer-like form that subsequently recurs in *The Crucifixion* (see pp. 52-53); the body has shrunk, as if drained of all its substance; and, finally, the shrillness of the colours (red, violet, yellow) that contrast with the black opening. The tension in this painting is further highlighted by the way in which the softness of the body and the armchair is counterbalanced by the architectural force of the composition, by the geometric framework that restricts the figure on either side.

The anatomical deformations inherited from the plastic exasperations of his monstrous Dinard bathers (see pp. 46-47) have led Picasso, as is shown in previous drawings also representing a woman in an armchair, to this expression of violence which reveals his ambiguous feelings towards women.

"He loves intensely, and he kills what he loves," Paul Éluard[3] is reported to have said, after the artist's handwriting was analysed. The 1927-1929 period was dominated by this disturbing, enigmatic image of women who were often portrayed as grotesque, threatening monsters. These visions allude to the marital discord between Pablo and Olga.

1. See *Guitar*, pp. 44-45.
2. André Fermigier, *Picasso*, Paris, Livre de Poche, 1969, p. 201.
3. Paul Éluard, in *Le Point*, vol. XLII, 1952, pp. 10-12.

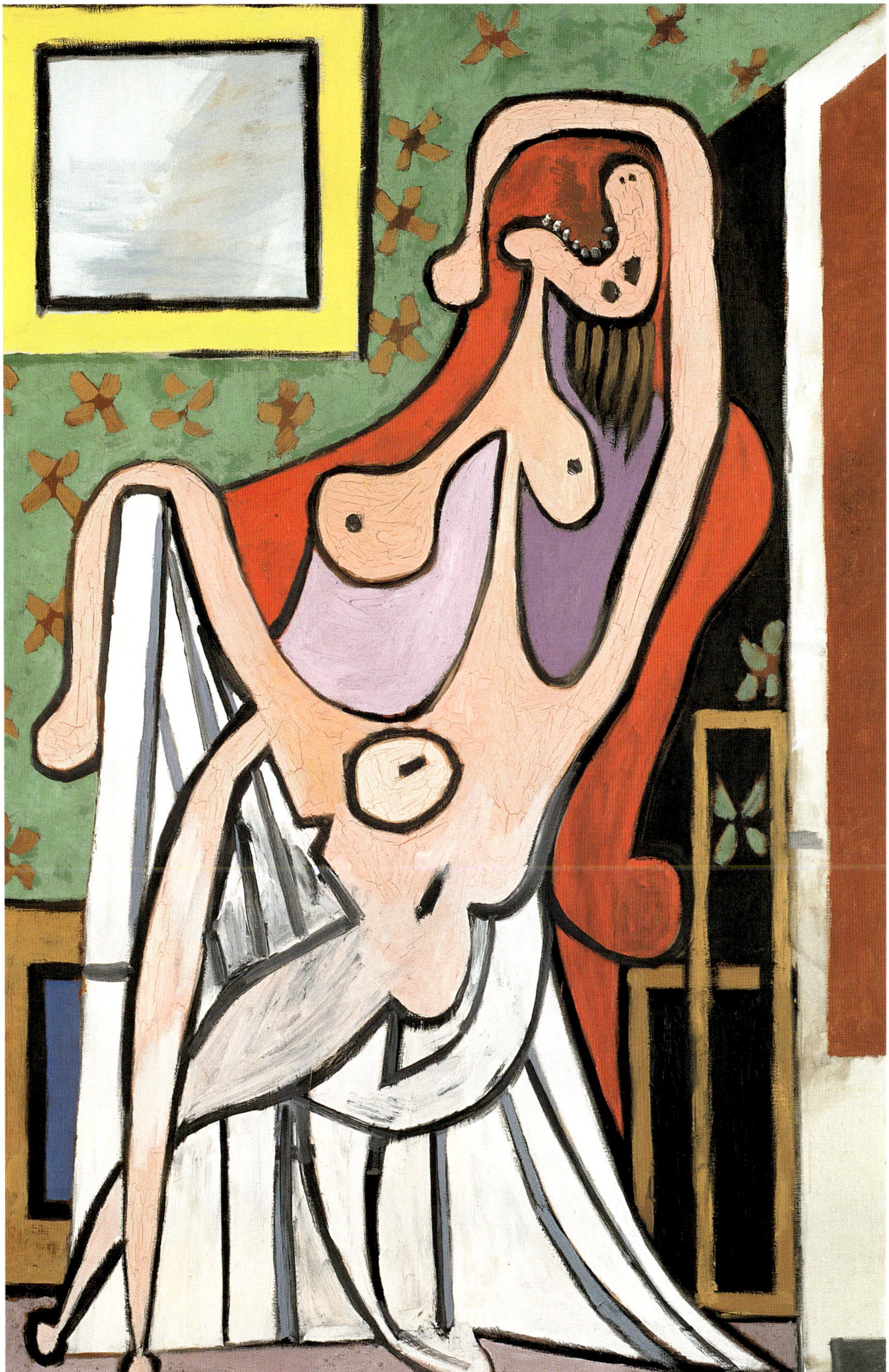

The Crucifixion

7 February 1930, Paris
Oil on plywood
51.5 x 66.5 cm
MP 122

Because of its religious subject, the complexity of its formal vocabulary and its strident colours, this is an exceptional painting in Picasso's oeuvre: chronologically situated between *Three Dancers* (1925, London, Tate Modern) and *Guernica* (1937, Madrid, Museo Reina Sofia), it is one of those fundamental works that epitomize the artist's universe and that has given rise to multiple interpretations. In his desire to regenerate the pictorial tradition, it was logical that Picasso would one day find himself confronted with this major theme from religious painting. While some of the Crucifixion's conventional motifs can be identified – Christ on the cross, the two small empty crosses (against a red background, on the right, and in the blue area, in the bottom left-hand corner), the bodies of the two thieves (also bottom left), the spear-bearer resembling a picador, the figure at the top of the ladder nailing Christ's hand to the cross and, lastly, the centurions playing dice on a drum for Christ's garment –, other figures have been added by Picasso, who has pieced together different motifs from earlier paintings like a puzzle.

The painting seems rather like a dictionary of the plastic vocabulary he used during the previous five years. The blue head of the praying mantis is that of the *Seated Bather* (1930, New York, Museum of Modern Art); the central white figure pressed up against Christ is that of the Virgin; her jagged-toothed mouth appeared in the *Large Nude in a Red Armchair* (see pp. 50-51), while her flat legs are those of the *Acrobat* (1930, Paris, Musée Picasso). The moonlike face shown in both frontal and profile views within a yellow triangle to the right of Christ, which is that of Marie-Thérèse Walter, comes from a painting dated November 1929 entitled *Head* (private collection).

Both a formal and an iconographic synthesis, this painting effectively combines the Crucifixion with other sources, such as the corrida and the theatre.The Crucifixion may be interpreted as a ritual sacrifice, close to the cult of Mithra, i.e. the sacrificial bull and solar symbolism. The colours are intimately linked to this theme, the blood red and the yellow sun contrasting with the pallid bodies of Christ and his mother and with the darkness that obscured the sky when Christ was put to death. The contorted figures with dislocated, intertwining limbs suggest the violence of an apocalyptic cataclysm.

Picasso would tackle this theme again in 1932, in a series of drawings made after Matthias Grünewald's *Crucifixion*.

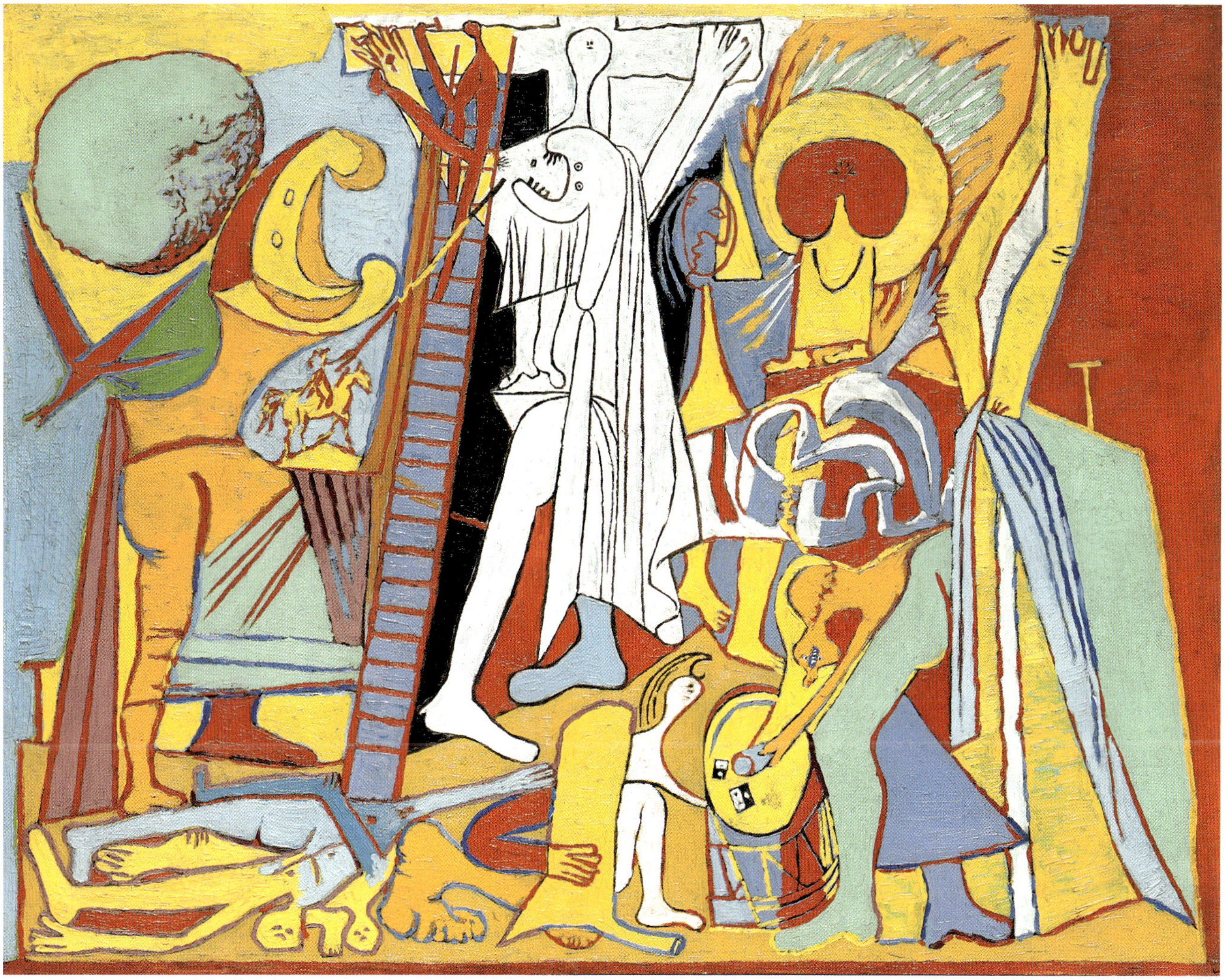

Relief Pictures in Sand

Standing Bather
14 August 1930,
Juan-les-Pins
Sand on the back of
a canvas and stretcher,
objects, cardboard, plant
matter sewn and glued
onto canvas
33 x 24.5 x 2 cm
MP 124

Face with
Two Profiles
14 August 1930,
Juan-les-Pins
Sand on the back of
a canvas and stretcher,
cardboard sewn and
glued onto canvas
41 x 33 x 1.5 cm
MP 126

Composition
with Glove
August 1930, Juan-les-Pins
Sand on the back of a
canvas and stretcher, glove,
fabric, cardboard, plant
matter sewn and glued
onto canvas
27.5 x 35.5 x 8 cm
MP 123

Poetic, Surrealist objects *par excellence*, these small *Relief Pictures* covered in sand form a complete and unique series in Picasso's oeuvre. Executed during the summer of 1930 in Juan-les-Pins, their materials – sand, objects found on the beach – and their themes – bathers and boats – testify to their place of creation and origin: once flotsam that rose from the deep and was cast up on the sand, they emerged from beneath the sand thanks to a treasure hunter of an artist. Picasso's fondness for found or discarded objects is well-known since he used them throughout his career: he chose these objects not only for their plastic, formal suggestiveness and their potential for metamorphosis, but also for their poetic evocativeness, their hidden meaning, and he juxtaposed them in bizarre combinations.

Most of the objects in these works can be found on the beach – twigs, string, scraps of old fabric, rubber ball, seaweed, palm leaves, toy boats, etc. Picasso mixed them with felt cutouts, sewed or glued them onto the back of a canvas, with the stretcher thus acting as an imitation frame, and then coated them in sand, which added unity to the work by concealing the differences in texture.

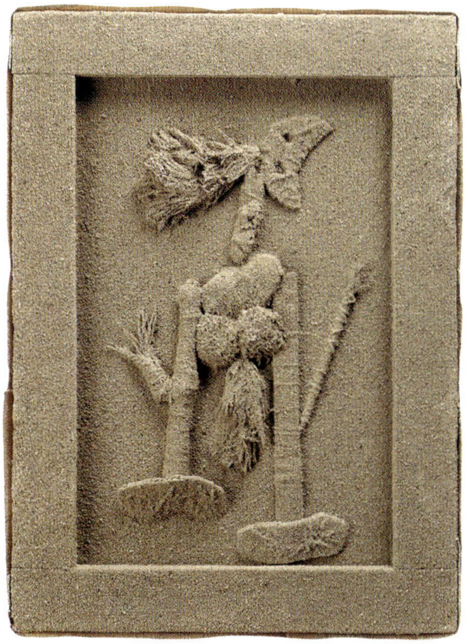
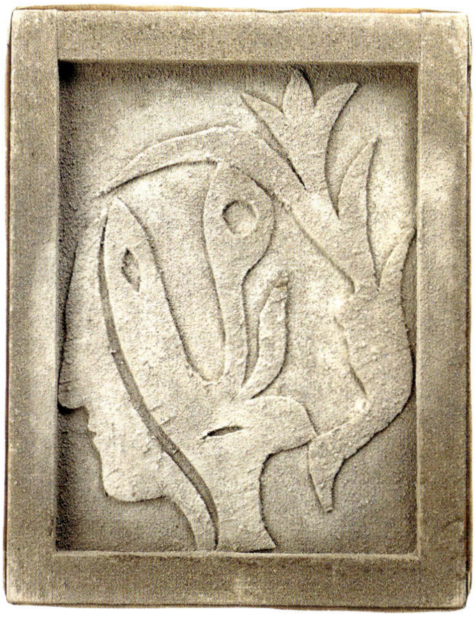
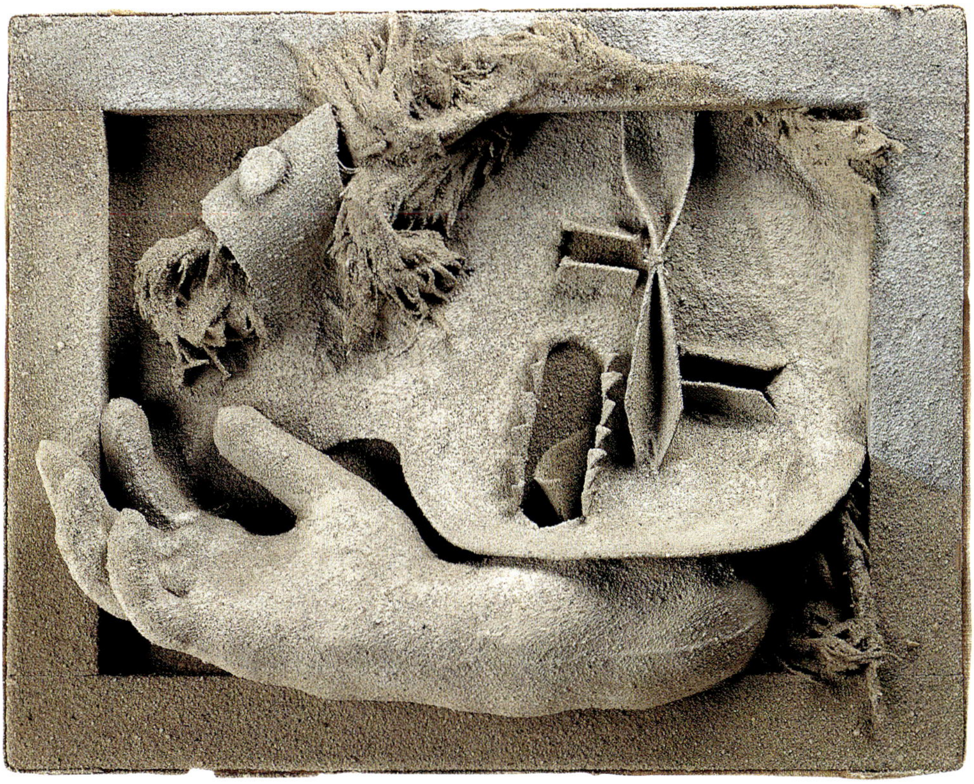

Figures at the Seashore

12 January 1931, Paris

Oil on canvas

130 x 195 cm

MP 131

Locked in their monstrous embrace, these strange, monumental *Figures at the Seashore* resembling petrified bones transport us into Picasso's world of phantasy and eroticism, while their imagery and symbolism illustrate the painter's affinities with Surrealism. They also give us a masterly demonstration of the inventiveness and evolution of the artist's plastic, formal vocabulary. With its warm golden light, its beige, ochre and pink tones, its seaside setting and beach hut, this painting belongs to the "Bathers" cycle executed in Cannes and Dinard (1927 and 1928-1929).

The erotic metaphors are evident here: faces reduced to wide, vagina-like mouths with pointed tongues darting between rows of teeth (Picasso was haunted by the idea of a *vagina dentata*), phallic nose, disjointed limbs and huge penis, all of which collide with each other and interpenetrate, like a set of building blocks complete with balls and levers, in a ferocious, unfaltering kiss. Since their attributes are all mixed up, the man can no longer be distinguished from the woman. The only identifiable organic forms – breasts, thighs, limbs – are reduced to smoothly polished, cylindroid monoliths, which transform the bodies into a monumental sculpture. The presence of the beach hut, a symbolic place which first appeared in the small Dinard paintings (see pp. 46-47), is an ironic reminder here of the contrast between civilization and the wild, primitive instincts of these prehistoric monsters.

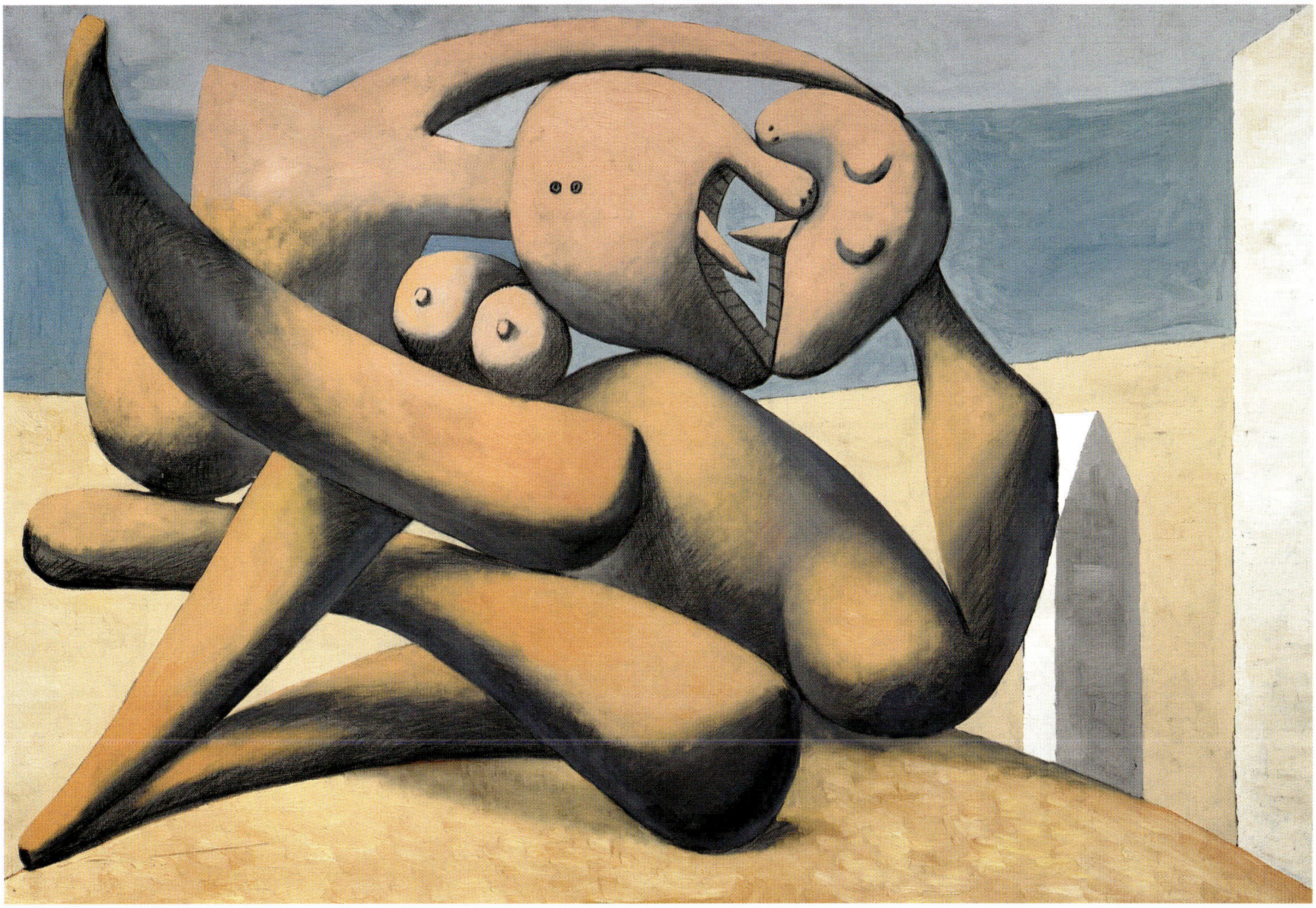

Still Life on a Pedestal Table

11 March 1931, Paris
Oil on canvas
195 x 130.5 cm
MP 134

"What a still life!" Picasso roared behind my back. "I always think we are going to see Marie-Thérèse..." I said. Picasso approached, and with his finger traced the profiles and curves that denoted Marie-Thérèse in his painting of 1931, scarcely changing any of the still life's rhythm. He turned around and slapped me on the shoulder: "That's why I still say, 'What a still life!'"[1]

In fact, few of Picasso's still lifes attained this monumentality, these exuberant colours, and it is easy to discern the veiled allusion to his latest mistress, Marie-Thérèse Walter, in the forms and choice of colours. The generosity of the rounded, curved forms, particularly the two green apples with black dots, the play of arabesques, and the dominant mauve and yellow tones are a striking reminder of the new pictorial language reserved for Marie-Thérèse that recur in works such as *Woman Reading* (1932, Paris, Musée Picasso) and *Reclining Nude* (see pp. 64-65). This language was inspired by her particular anatomy and Picasso's return to in-the-round sculpture since purchasing a new studio at Boisgeloup, near Gisors.

From the conventional still-life theme, Picasso retained the following motifs: the three-legged pedestal table, which can also be seen in Georges Braque's large *Still Lifes with Pedestal Table*, the white compotier with three pieces of fruit, and the big yellow pitcher whose form strangely recalls the one that emerges out of the capricious lines in *The Painter and his Model* (1926, see pp. 42-43). Everything seems to move and undulate in this painting which overflows with vitality – the twisted table legs, the sinuous volutes, the swirling lines of the floor and wall, nothing can resist the dynamic energy of the play of curves. The ovoid or genital organic forms – the fruit or the stem of the compotier, the table legs – are images of fertility closely related to Picasso's vision of Marie-Thérèse: that of a plant-like woman ready to blossom, from whom flowers and fruit may burst forth, as is seen in other portraits dating to this time, *Nude in a Garden* (see pp. 70-71) or *Reclining Nude*. The continuous black line was previously found in *The Kiss* (see pp. 40-41) and *The Painter and his Model*. Here it encloses flat areas of bright, bold colour in the way lead is used in stained-glass windows, the luminosity of which this painting shares.

1. Pierre Daix, *La Vie de peintre de Pablo Picasso*, Paris, Le Seuil, 1977, p. 231.

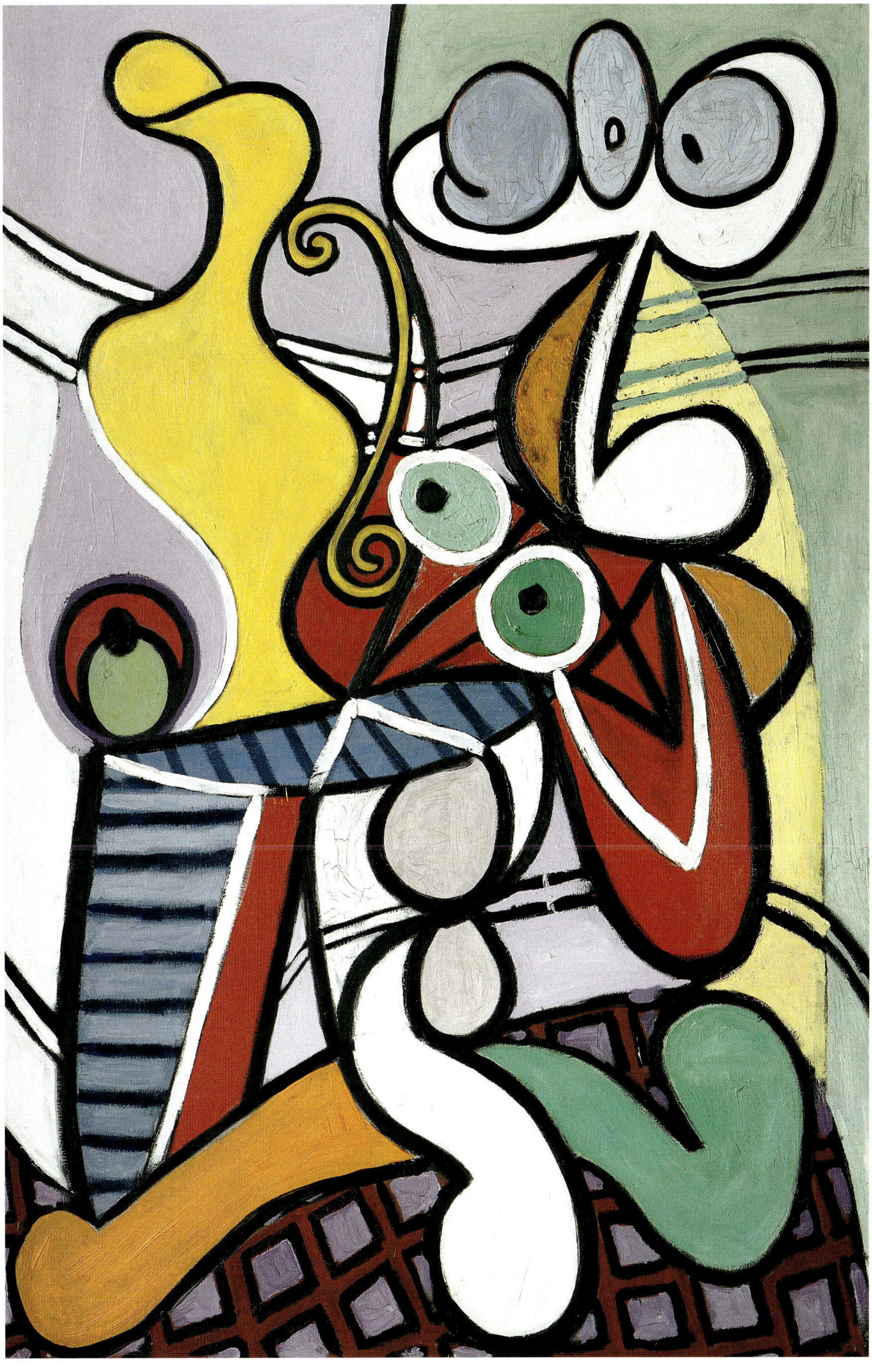

Composition with a Butterfly

1932, Boisgeloup
Fabric, wood, plant matter, string, drawing pin, butterfly and oil on canvas
16 x 22 x 2.5 cm
MP 1982-169

A drawing pin, a few matches, a scrap of fabric, a piece of string, a leaf from a lime tree and a butterfly, glued onto a painted canvas partially coated in a creamy white lacquer which avoids the insect's fragile, mottled wings and the veins of the leaf, the only indications of life in this artistic composition... This was how Picasso used the most ordinary, discarded objects to create the small masterpiece that had such an effect on André Breton, this poetic picture in which the marvellous is ensnared as if by magic in reality.

On the left is a figure with a drawing pin for a head, bits of wood for arms and legs and a scrap of material for the body; on the right is another figure teased out of a length of string; between the two is the leaf, the plant motif chosen for its fine, light texture and symbolism, and the real butterfly, delicately placed on the canvas with a trail of bristles caught in the paint behind it. "It is the first time," said André Breton in 1932, "that an actual butterfly has been included in the field of a picture and that he was able to do it without everything that surrounded it immediately crumbling into dust, without the disconcerting representations that its presence here might provoke being detrimental to the system of human representations in which it is incorporated."[1]

The picture is illuminated by the unusual presence of the butterfly and the latter takes flight again by emerging from the canvas.

1. André Breton, "Picasso dans son élément," in *Minotaure*, no. 1, 1933.

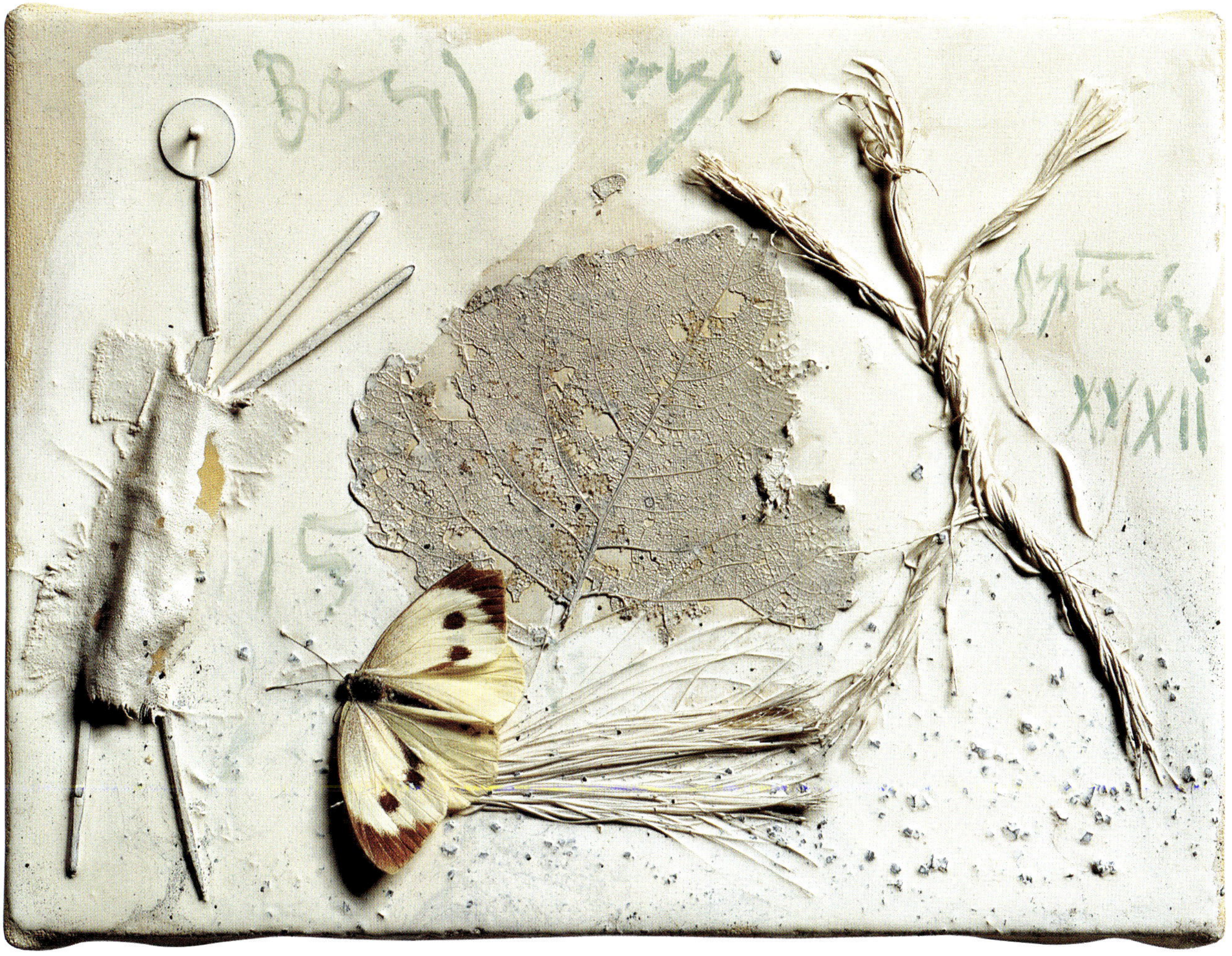

Woman in a Red Armchair

27 January 1932, Boisgeloup

Oil on canvas

130.2 x 97 cm

MP 138

"I have a veritable passion for bones... I have lots of others at Boisgeloup: skeletons of bird, heads of dogs and sheep... I've even got a rhinoceros skull... Have you ever noticed that bones are always modelled not carved, that one always has the impression that they've come out of a mould after being modelled in clay? And have you ever noticed how their convex and concave forms fit together? And how skilfully the vertebrae are "adjusted" to one another?"[1]

Pablo Picasso

Is this a painting of a sculpture or a painted sculpture? A picture like *Woman in a Red Armchair* reveals both the essential dialogue that Picasso constantly maintained between these two means of expression, and, more specifically, the nature of the relationship existing between them, i.e. the aspiration towards volume and real space. From the time of the anatomic metamorphoses in the Cannes and Dinard "Bathers" (1927 and 1928-1929), which Picasso had already interpreted in sculpture (*Metamorphoses I and II*, 1928, Paris, Musée Picasso), "the parts of the body stretched out and tended to form autonomous volumes, which could soon be treated in detached fragments suitable for composing bodies or the equivalents of bodies through the assemblage of cylindroid masses, forcefully calling for the rolling movement of their modelling to complete itself in a volume."[2] Derived from the monolithic forms of *Figures at the Seashore* (see pp. 56-57), this pile of bones, which represents the different parts of the female body, heralds the variations on Matthias Grünewald's *Crucifixion* that Picasso was to execute, in which the human body is reduced to its final skeletal state, a bony framework, a mechanical object.

Here Picasso subjects the woman to the most radical stylistic manipulations. Her slightly reclining pose recalls that of Marie-Thérèse in contemporary paintings. The head's round eyes are similar to those in the sculpture *Head* (1932, Paris, Musée Picasso). The woman's arms, neck and spherical breasts and abdomen can be identified, while her back merges into that of the armchair, which is itself broken up into separate volumes. The dramatization of the painting inherent in the morbid representation of the face is heightened by the red and black tones and the chalky, white light. The presence of bones in Picasso's oeuvre may be explained in several ways – because of the artist's personal taste, his formal, plastic logic, and, of course, the morbidity of the related symbolism.

1. Brassaï, *Conversations avec Picasso*, Gallimard, 1964, p. 94.
2. Max Loreau, "Picasso: du volume en peinture", in *Poésie*, no. 15, 1980, p. 55.

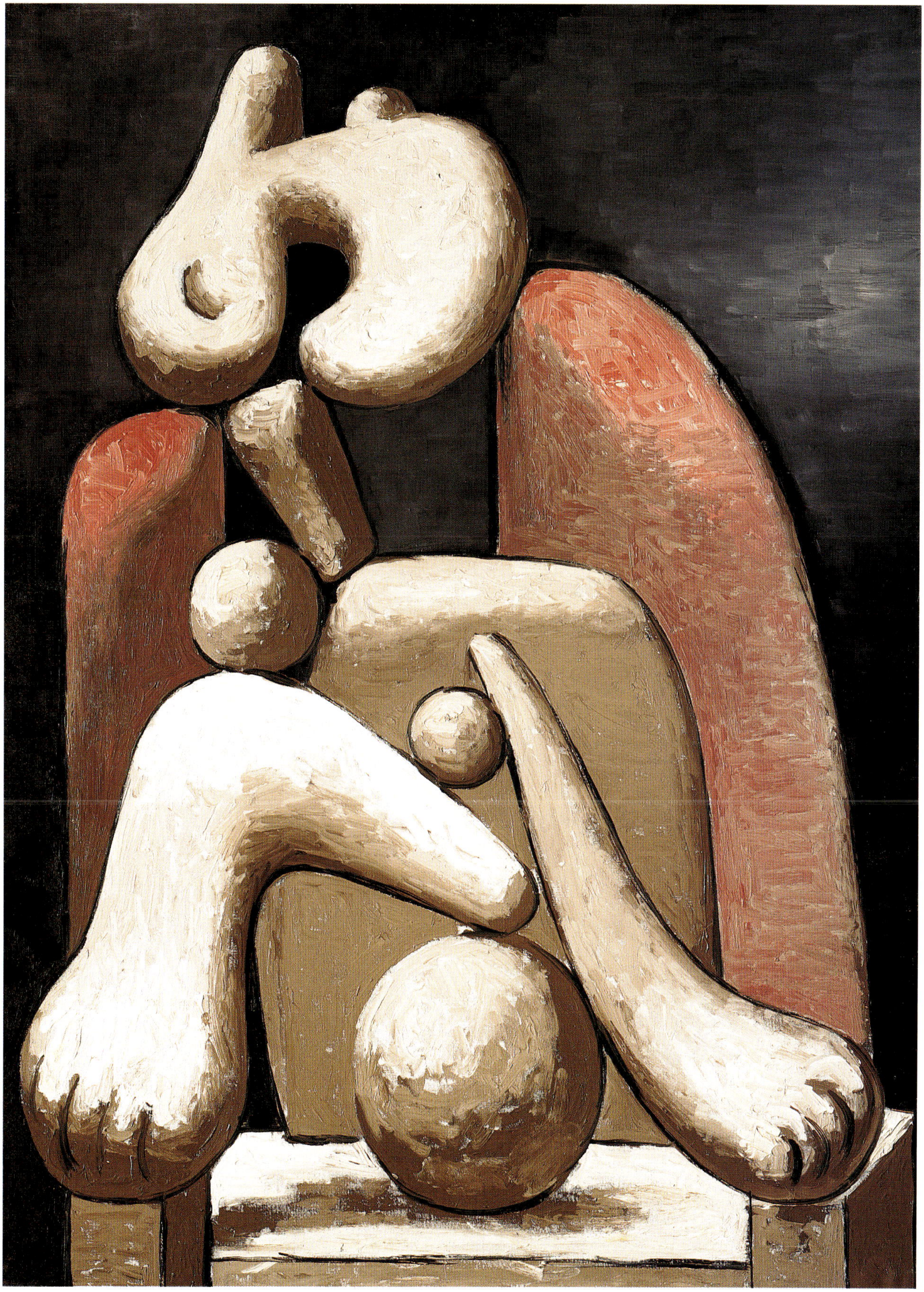

Reclining Nude

4 April 1932, Boisgeloup

Oil on canvas

130 x 161.7 cm

MP 142

From 1931 to 1936, Marie-Thérèse Walter, a young, seventeen-year-old girl encountered by chance in the street in 1927, invaded Picasso's painting and sculpture. Long kept secret in the painter's private life, she was, however, omnipresent in his art. Picasso seemed to have been meant to meet her and it was therefore his foresight that urged him to immediately declare on seeing her: "We're going to do great things together." From that moment on, his painting dreamt of plasticity, volume and modelling and Marie-Thérèse's vital, rounded, sculptural forms corresponded perfectly to his desire to explore modelling and freestanding sculpture. She gave rise to a colourful new formal vocabulary, which was a logical progression from the Cannes and Dinard period.

The very matt white highlights, rubbed roughly like pastel over the body and the background, are used here to render the modelling of the forms and confer an exceptional luminosity upon *Reclining Nude*. The woman's nudity seems to bathe in powdery sunlight, in sulphurous, yellow warmth. The intensity of the light beams is suggested by the brightness of the sun and the decorative motifs in the background. The sensual, voluptuous arabesques of the body curled up in a figure of eight are somewhat reminiscent of Henri Matisse's *Blue Nude* and recur in a sculpture dating to the same period (*Reclining Bather*, Paris, Musée Picasso).

As in *Still Life on a Pedestal Table* (see pp. 58-59), Picasso associates female sexuality with organic fertilization in the vegetable kingdom and images of fecundity and maturation, evoked here by the two pears, breasts ressembling ripe fruit, broad green leaves and the kidney-bean-shaped head enclosed in an egg.

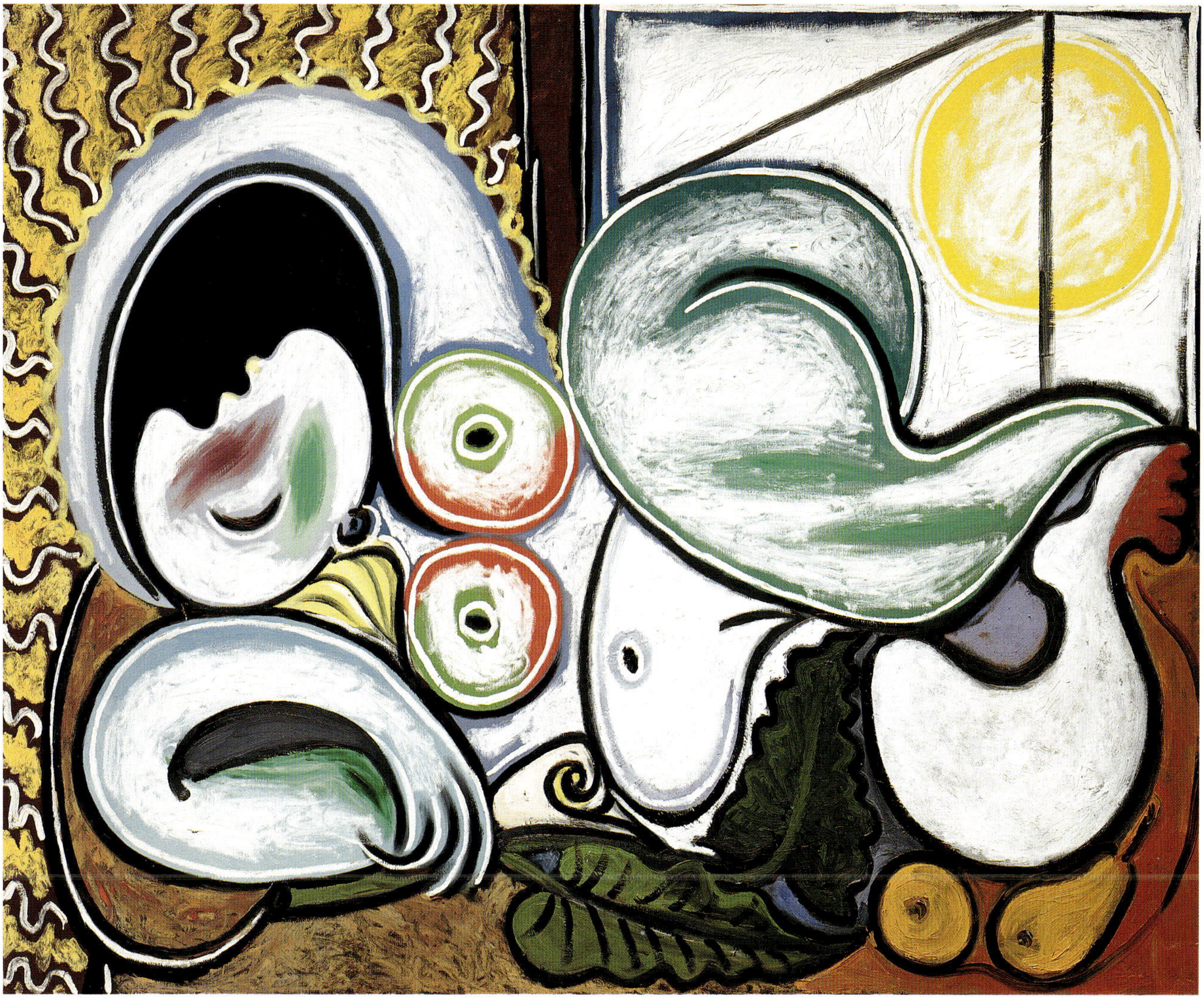

The Corrida – The Death of the Torero

19 September 1933,
Boisgeloup
Oil on wood
31 x 40 cm
MP 145

A full-blooded Spaniard and out-and-out *aficionado*, Picasso was the painter of bullfights *par excellence*. Distant childhood memories took him back to the arenas of Malaga, accompanied by his father, and his early paintings were dedicated to the theme; each return visit to Spain would give rise to new corridas. Everything about this theme appealed to him: not only the vibrant spectacle with its bright, shimmering colours and strong contrast between light and shadow, but also, and above all, the bloody sacrificial rite in which man and beast, bull and horse, the symbolic couple whose duality is equivalent to that of man and woman, are pitted against each other in a tragic, mortal combat. For Picasso, the bull is in fact the symbol of masculinity and virility, while the horse with its gaping entrails represents womanhood – relationships based not simply on violence, brutality and possession, but also pleasure and exaltation, which would recur in the "Minotaur" series and which convey the ambiguity of Picasso's eroticism.

In a whirl of flamboyant, scintillating colours dominated by blood red, bright pink and golden yellow, the black bull lifts and frenetically bears away the dead torero together with the white, disembowelled horse that twists back its neck in a terrified gesture and a shriek of agony. The centripetal movement, whereby the limbs of the figures radiate from the middle of the canvas, is created by the elliptical form of the bull, the broad curve of whose back follows that of the arena. The vertiginous impact of the fall is suggested by the torero's ecstatic, reclining pose, similar to the attitude of abandon found in the companion piece executed the same year, *Death of the Female Torero* (Paris, Musée Picasso).

This close-up view of the scene invades the entire picture space. The different handling of the two parts – one extremely detailed with a powerful use of relief, the other flat and sketchlike – heightens the effect of instability and hurls the bull forward.

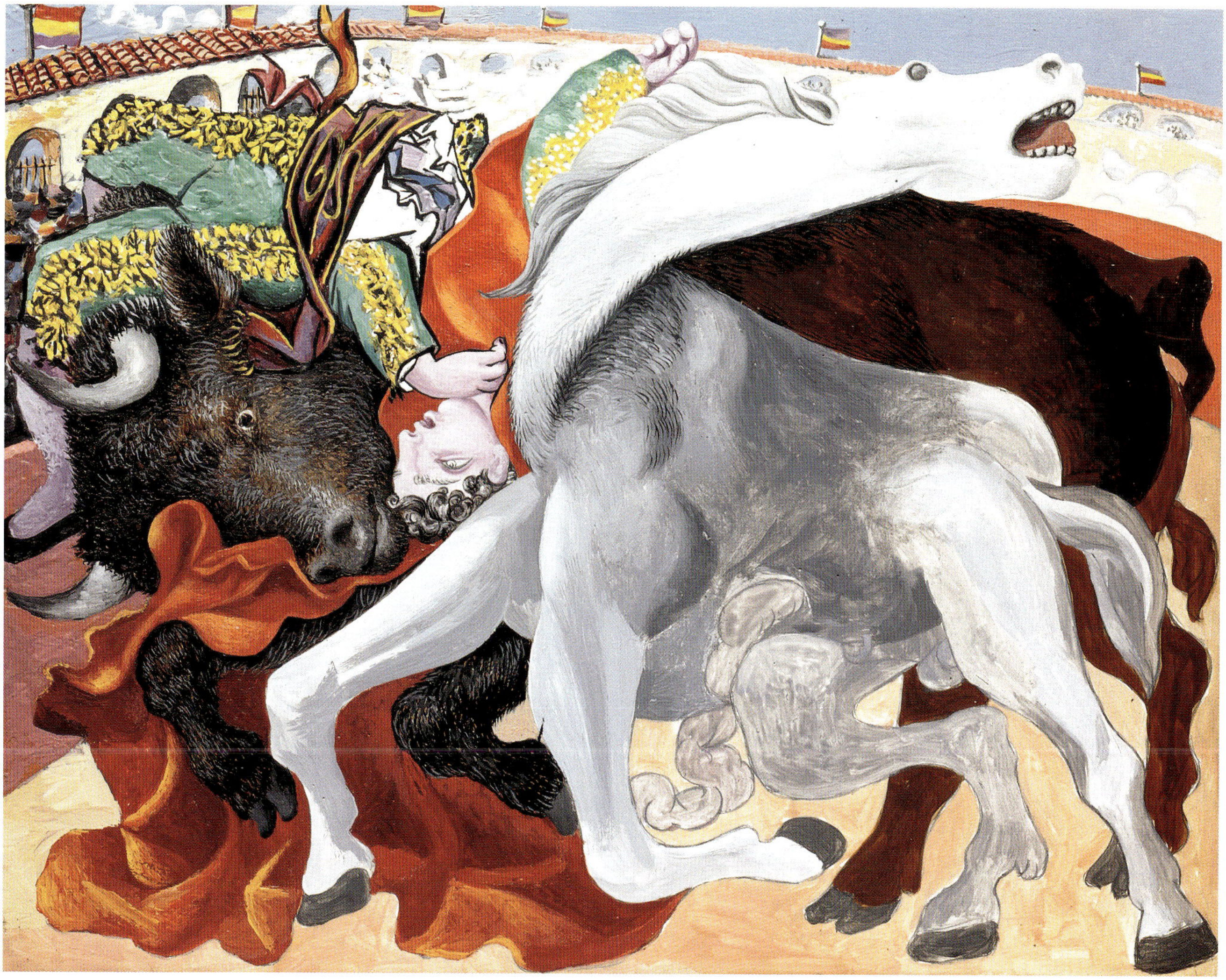

Woman with Leaves

1934, Boisgeloup

Bronze (unique piece)

37.9 x 20 x 25.9 cm

MP 314

Reminiscent of an ancient effigy, *Woman with Leaves* is the most mysterious and impressive figure in Picasso's sculptures from this period. The combination of commonplace and incongruous characteristics with hieratic solemnity reveals the genius of an artist who, using poetry and humour, transformed the humblest materials into ritual gestures and eternal figures. As in *Woman Leaning on her Elbows* (1933), *Bearded Figure* (1933), *Woman with an Orange* (1934) and *The Orator* (1937), all four of which are now in the Musée Picasso, Paris, the artist moulded the texture on certain parts of the body and used modelling techniques to assemble the whole piece. He poured plaster in or on objects – here, corrugated cardboard for the body, a matchbox for the head, beech leaves for an arm –, thus obtaining on the surface the imprint of the texture of the material used. The original plaster sculpture was then cast in bronze, so as to unite this assemblage of disparate elements in a noble medium.

One of the interesting aspects of this type of sculpture is the way in which the spectator has to decipher which discarded objects have been used. The choice of these elements was not purely accidental: the grooves in the corrugated cardboard evoke the pleats in drapery; the fine network of veins in the leaves interplay with the machine-made lines of the cardboard; the rectangular matchbox transforms the face into an inscrutable mask. "Square heads because they should be round."[1] Despite her rigidity, this oracular figure is incredibly vivacious. "She seems to vibrate with the rustling of leaves, with the swish of the folds of her garment."[2] Finally, the body's association with the plant world, a constant in Picasso's art during this period, should also be noted.

1. André Malraux, *La Tête d'obsidienne*, Paris, Gallimard, 1974, p. 29.
2. Werner Spies, *Les Sculptures de Picasso*, Lausanne, Clairefontaine, 1971, p. 141.

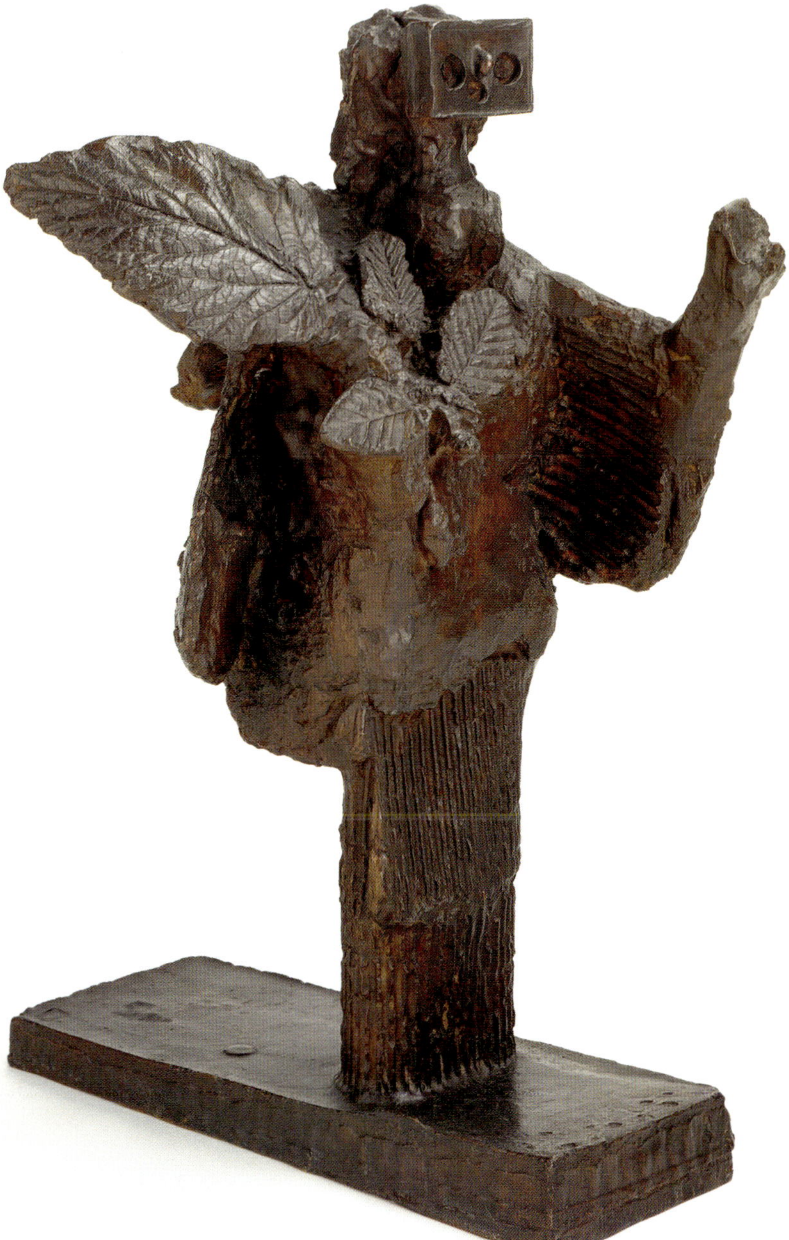

Nude in a Garden

4 August 1934, Boisgeloup

Oil on canvas

162 x 130 cm

MP 148

In this other nude, much later than the *Reclining Nude* of 1932 (see pp. 64-65), Picasso takes the transformation of Marie-Thérèse Walter's body even further and, consequently, goes even further in his painting. In fact, it seems as if everything here is "painted"; the traces of hasty brush-strokes, the use of impasto and superimposed layers of paint and the transparency revealing the artist's frenzy and exaltation confer an exceptional materiality upon the work. The evolution from a sculptural, sketch-like vision (*Reclining Nude*) to a wholly pictorial vision – more fluid yet with thickly applied pigment – is similar to that which occurred between *Figures at the Seashore* (see pp. 56-57) and *Woman Throwing a Stone* (1931, Paris, Musée Picasso).

Together, the colours, the medium and the forms are a hymn to Marie-Thérèse, as if the desired body incarnated the painting – the bright pink of the flesh, the lush green of the foliage, the grey-blue of the water and the red and gold of the oriental cushion. The curled-up body is reduced to an ovoid form; the bean-pod-shaped blonde hair, the flowers, plants and watery element again evoke images of fecundity. The necklace from which a long, lithe neck emerges adds a lunar profile to the breast at the same time. The suppleness and grace of this female nude cannot fail to recall Henri Matisse's painting.

This concept of a flowerlike, plantlike woman, a nourishing, seeded land, within which the biological mystery of procreation and life is performed, has its origins in the most ancient archetypes and is facilitated by the state of sleep. Freed of the constraints of consciousness, the "dream" body metamorphoses into its primitive organic state and abandons itself to all erotic phantasies. For Picasso, Marie-Thérèse was always the supreme example of "the woman who sleeps", revealing and surrendering herself to the painter's gaze.

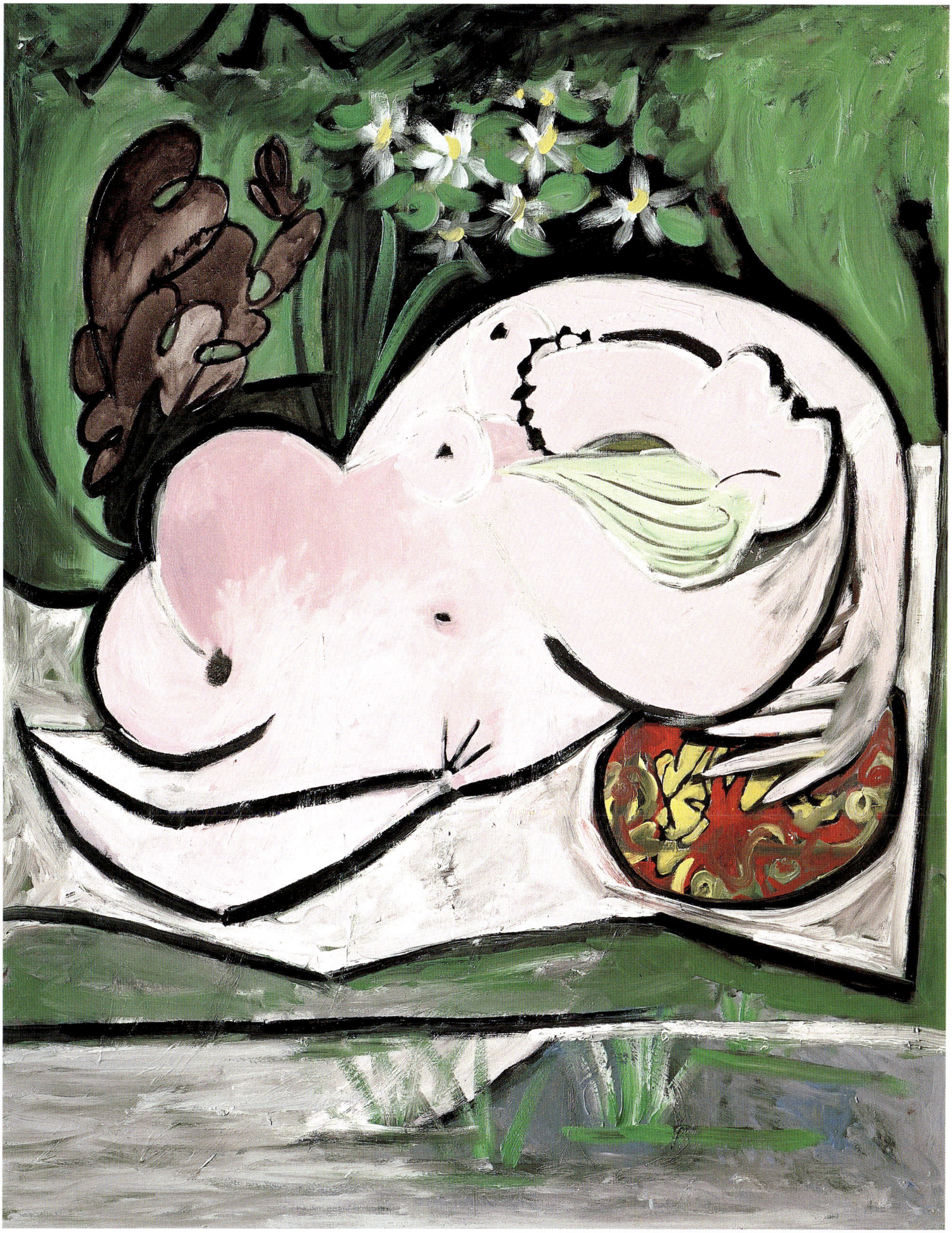

Straw Hat with Blue Leaves

1 May 1936, Juan-les-Pins
Oil on canvas
61 x 50 cm
MP 155

Is this a still life or a woman's face? Picasso takes the dislocation of the human figure to extremes here. The triangle of pink flesh, with its two large semicircular eyes and twisted nose and mouth, is superimposed on a long, mauve, vase-shaped neck, on top of which is a hat folded into a figure of eight and adorned with blue foliage. This neck emerges from a yellow and grey border that may be interpreted as the picture frame.

Such disorganization of the face, which in no way diminishes its physiognomy or expressiveness, was often seen as Picasso's need to be destructive and aggressive towards women. In fact, the artist treats the face and body as objects to be deconstructed and reassembled according to the plastic laws specific to his painting. If the work were completely abstract, i.e. without identifiable organs, the visual impact would be less striking. The image achieves its provocative, angry, humorous, derisory objective because of the humanity and expressivity that remain in these incongruous forms.

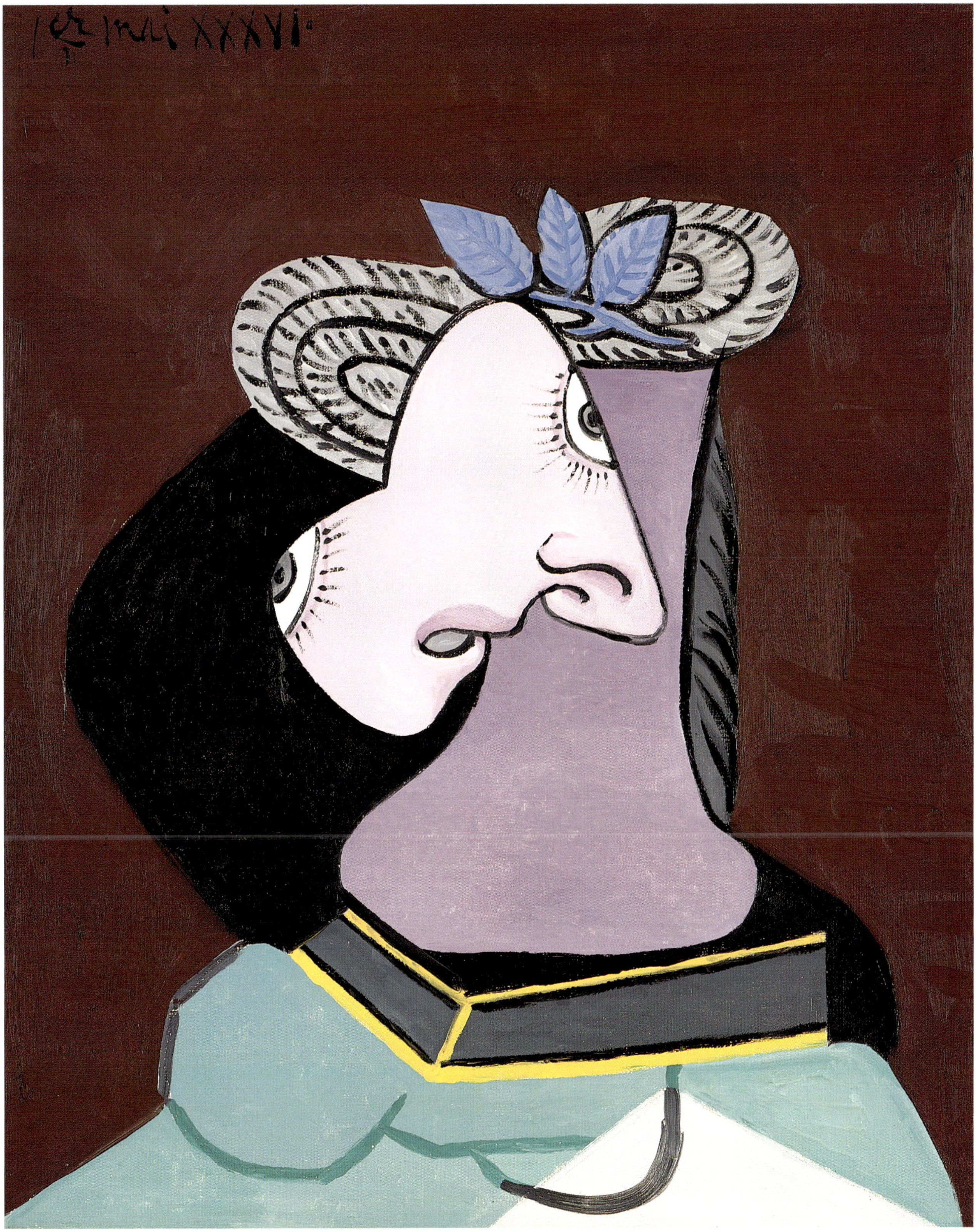
1er mai XXXVI

The Minotaur and Dead Mare in front of a Cave

6 May 1936, Juan-les-Pins
Gouache and Indian ink
on paper
50 x 65.5 cm
MP 1163

The Minotaur – a legendary and tragic dimension of Mediterranean culture – is a central theme in Picasso's universe. "If one marked on a map all the itineraries along which I had travelled, and if one joined them up with a line, that would perhaps represent a Minotaur," he himself once said. This mythological figure is without doubt the most powerful and the most laden with conscious or subconscious significance in his entire oeuvre. The spatial configuration of the labyrinth, the bridge between two cultures, uniting the Mithra cult and the corrida, Pasiphae's son and the Spanish *toro*, the Minotaur, with whom Picasso identified completely, is the very symbol of duality – duality of the work, of being, of creation. Half-man, half-beast, he at once embodies the monster, primitive bestiality, the obscure forces of the subconscious, executioner and victim, love and death.

In this gouache, the Minotaur holds the drooping body of a mare in his arms and raises his hand, in a gesture similar to that found in the famous engraving entitled *The Minotauromachy* (1935, Paris, Musée Picasso), to wave away the young woman crowned with flowers who is watching him from behind her veil and whose arm seems to be imprisoned in a huge plaster cast. On the left, the dark cave, from which two imploring hands emerge, may recall the exit from the labyrinth and a tearful Ariadne. The Minotaur with such a human face, expressing deep sadness, is Picasso, while the disembowelled mare is Marie-Thérèse Walter.

The complex combination of themes, which are open to numerous and varied interpretations, fills the scene with mystery and confers a poetic dimension upon it.

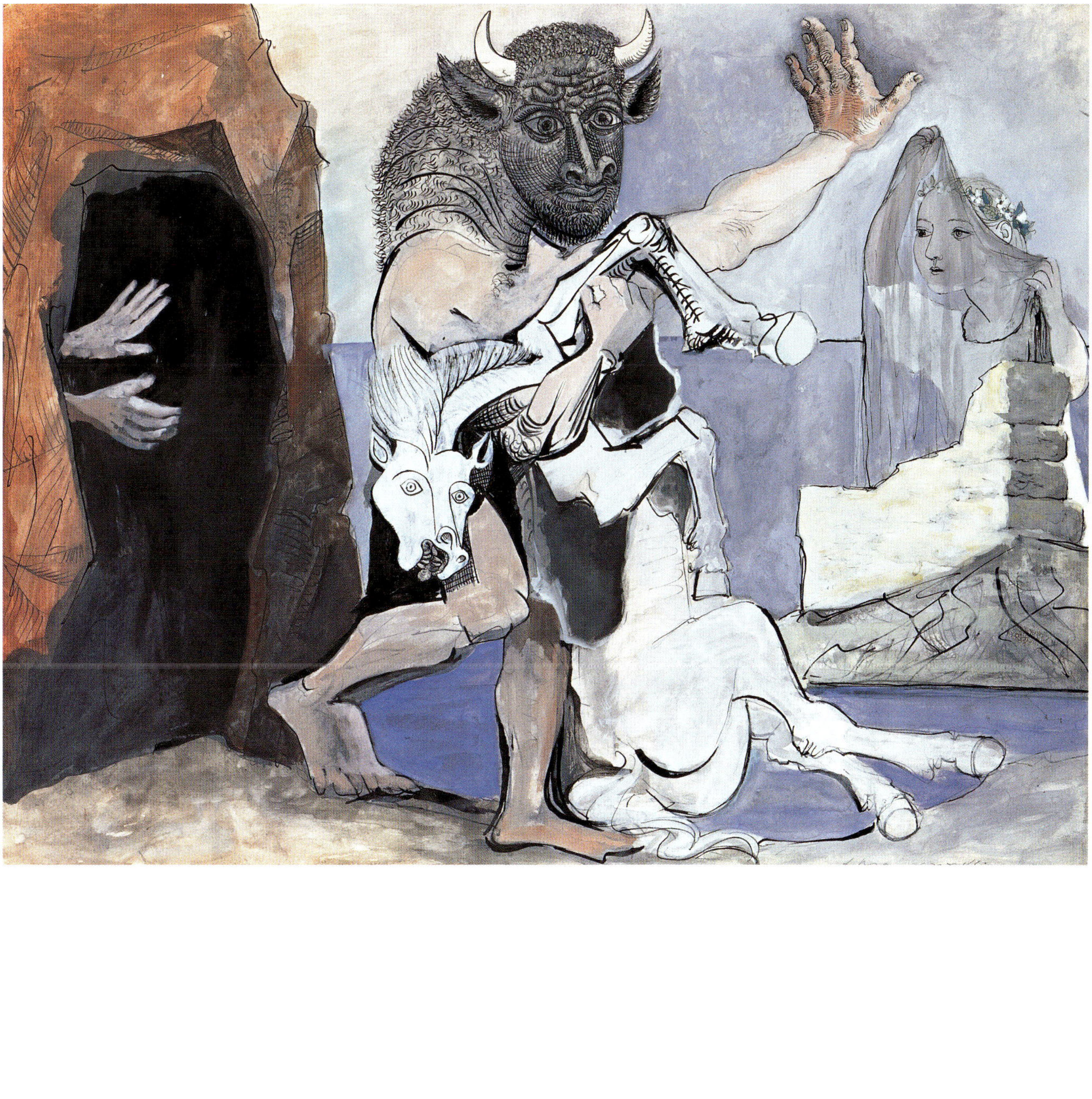

Dora and the Minotaur (Composition)

5 September 1936, Paris
Graphite pencil, wax crayons, ink and scratchings on paper
40.5 x 72 cm
MP 1998-308

Having been introduced in a large collage (Paris, Musée National d'Art Moderne) in 1928, the Minotaur reappeared in 1933, brandishing his sceptre like a phallic dagger, on the cover of the first issue of the magazine *Minotaure*. Further adventures of Picasso and the Minotaur then served as the theme of a series of engravings known as the *Suite Vollard*, a whole chapter of which is devoted to lovemaking, feasting and the creature's death in the arena. Picasso's interpretation of the ancient myth was relatively free. A series of drawings executed at this time highlighted the eroticism of the coupling between bull and woman, an amorous struggle that for the artist ranked alongside the sexual encounter between bull and horse. Roles may interchange, slipping from man to beast, from beast to human, yet the protagonists in most of these drawings and engravings are Picasso and Marie-Thérèse Walter.

But in September 1936, the artist met Dora Maar and she took the place usually reserved for Marie-Thérèse. This work, which never left Dora Maar's collection, probably because the model drawn so delicately was easily recognizable, was only discovered at the posthumous sale of her estate. Her face is effectively the only thing that remains intact in this fiery embrace, reflected by incandescent Nature. The erotic scene is set in a landscape with a blazing sky and bushes flattened by the weight of the entwined bodies. In the background, a sort of grove or treehouse with a ladder is visible, which recalls the motif used on the stage curtain in *Parade* (1917), or that in *The Crucifixion* (see pp. 52-53) or in *Minotauromachy* (1935, Paris, Musée Picasso). Thrown on her back, with limbs twisted and body bent in two, the woman's acrobatic position as she lies trapped between the Minotaur's arms and thighs expresses the violence of desire and the feelings not only of attraction and tenderness but also the cruelty binding the monster here to his "victim".

The technique is particularly interesting for Picasso used three sheets of juxtaposed paper and vehemently scratched the support to make the drawing more expressive

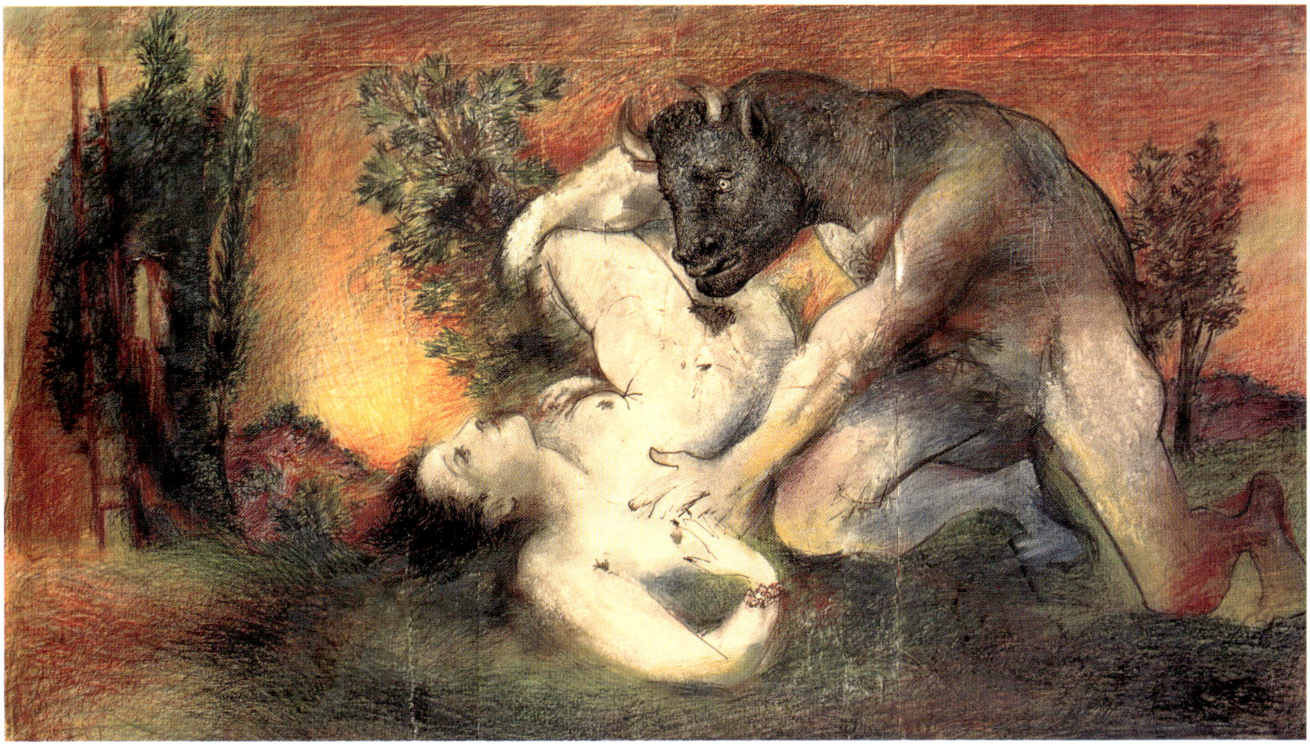

Portrait of Dora Maar

1937, Paris
Oil on canvas
92 x 65 cm
MP 158

In 1936, a new woman entered Picasso's life – Dora Markovitch. A young photographer of Yugoslav origin, she spoke Spanish, was a friend of Paul Éluard and was involved in the Surrealist movement. From then on, for a period of several years, the figures of the two muses – Dora the brunette and Marie-Thérèse the blonde – alternated in Picasso's painting.

In this dazzling portrait full of sumptuous colours, Dora, seated majestically in an armchair, her head resting on a long, slender hand with painted fingernails, has a faint smile on her lips. Her face is shown in frontal and profile views; a red eye looks in one direction, a green eye looks in another... all these deformations are essential characteristics of Picasso's art. And yet, despite these distortions, or perhaps because of them, the artist succeeds in producing a strikingly true-to-life likeness. There was an expressive objective in all these deformations: it was not so much a question of reconstructing reality, but rather of expressing all its possibilities, of simultaneously depicting his model from all angles. All pictorial means were thus used to "express" Dora, her physique, her temperament, and the painter's vision of her. Some of the model's distinctive features can easily be recognized: the red fingernails, the long, slender, graceful hands, the pose, the black hair, the dark, staring eyes, the round, determined chin and the black, laced-up, embroidered blouse, which can also be seen in an eponymous work from the same year (Paris, Musée Picasso). Her eyes sparkle with intelligence and vivacity and she has a smiling, distant expression on her face, whose relief effects are achieved through a play of light and colour that turn her cheek into a peach. The tapering, pointed forms of her blouse and fingers express elegance and distinction, while the cross-shaped motifs on the armchair and the embroidery, together with the check pattern on her skirt and the horizontal and vertical stripes of the background, which evoke a monk's cell or the bars of a prison, suggest that the figure has been enclosed in a cruel, restricted mental space.

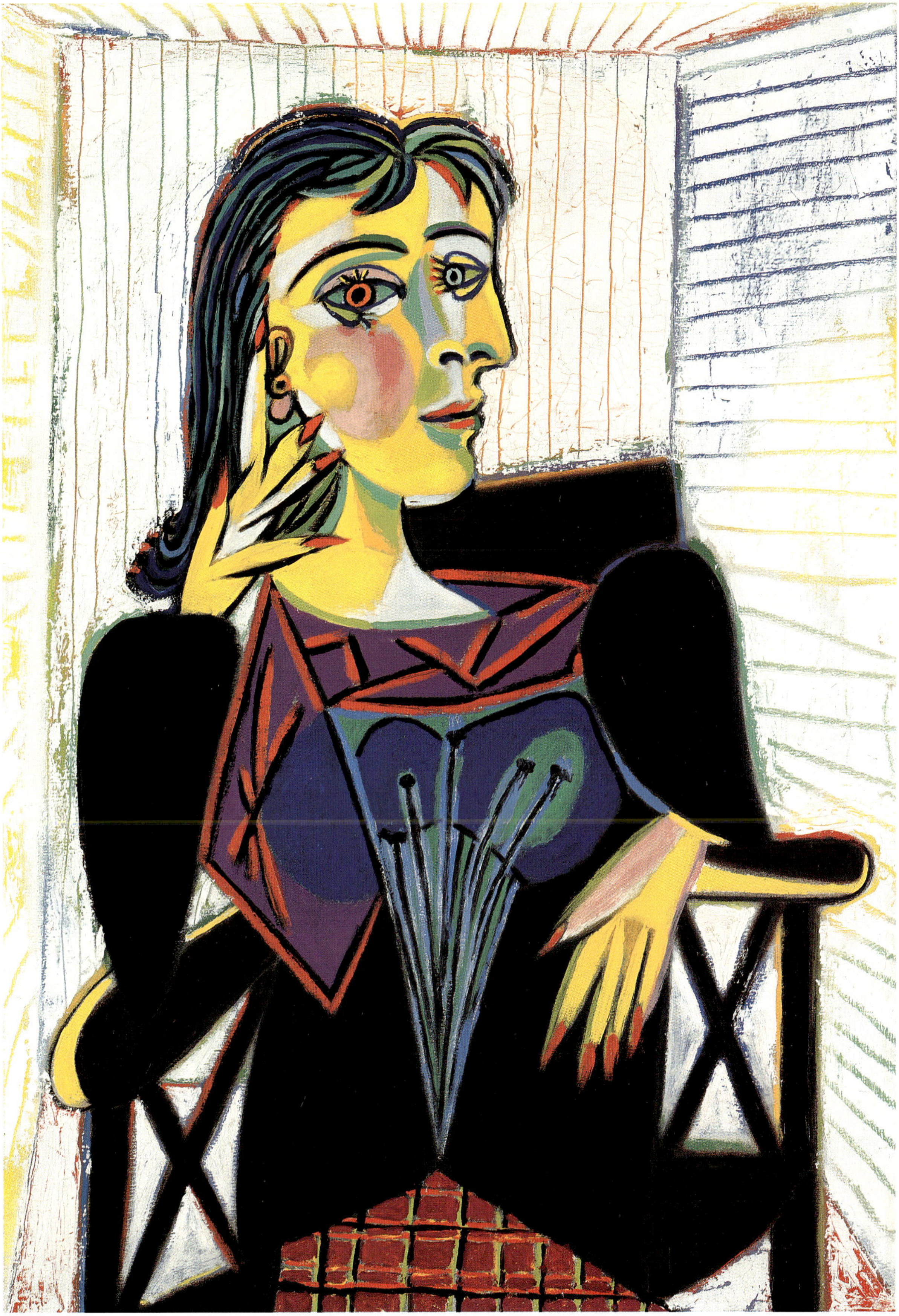

Portrait of Marie-Thérèse Walter

6 January 1937, Paris

Oil on canvas

100 x 81 cm

MP 159

While the pictorial language reserved for Dora Maar was often governed by angular forms and contrasting reds and blacks, the one Picasso used for Marie-Thérése Walter, as in the Boisgeloup period, continued to employ rounded contours, soft colours, arabesques and pastel shades dominated by yellows and blues. Here, her body is lithe and she has long palmate fingers. Her face is bathed in cold blue and green tones that create a dreamlike atmosphere of poetic reverie and tenderness. The striped motif, evocative of corrugated cardboard, contrasts with the bare simplicity of the background which, since it is out of perspective, resembles a box. The large nose jutting out from the line of the forehead, Marie-Thérèse's distinctive facial feature, and the eyes popping through the slotted eyelids like coins are easily recognizable. The deformation of the face is more a plastic distortion here than a combination of frontal and profile views.

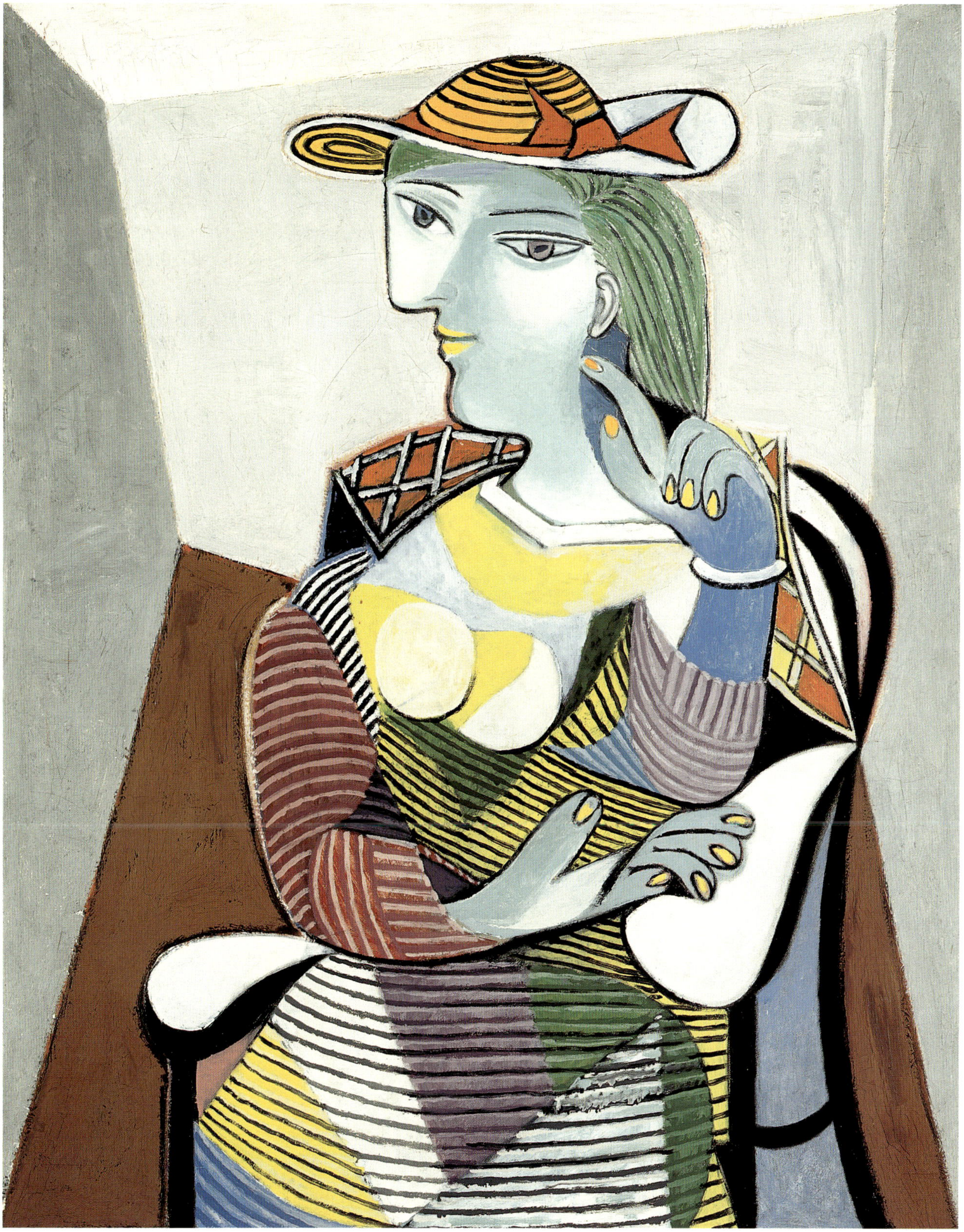

Bather with a Book

18 February 1937, Paris
Oil, pastel and charcoal
on canvas
130 x 97.5 cm
MP 160

Here again is the beach, the sea and a female bather's naked body, but now the full, smooth volumes of 1931 have hardened, become geometrical, and the combination of cants, solids and hollows recalls the Cubist system of construction. With its alternating curved forms and sharp edges, the body is rigorously structured and air flows between pillar-like arms.

Picasso entered a new phase in his "Bathers" cycle with this picture. The erotic aspect has disappeared and made way for familiar scenes full of humour, imagination and mystery. This stage also includes a more monstrous scene, *Two Nude Women on the Beach* (1937, Paris, Musée Picasso), reminiscent of his Dinard series. These two paintings were not produced during a Mediterranean holiday, but were executed in his new studio at Tremblay-sur-Mauldre, or in the Rue des Grands-Augustins, Paris. The seascape, which offers a harmonious, neutral space, was thus chosen to set off the figure's three-dimensional volume.

The pink, grey and blue tones, scored with white, and the powdery pastel make the body look rough and friable. Picasso plays on the morphological ambiguity of some of the limbs: the left arm, for example, might be seen as a figure. The form of the book is also handled in a particular manner: it looks like a triangular block of stone, while the words written on it resemble the lines of a thumbprint.

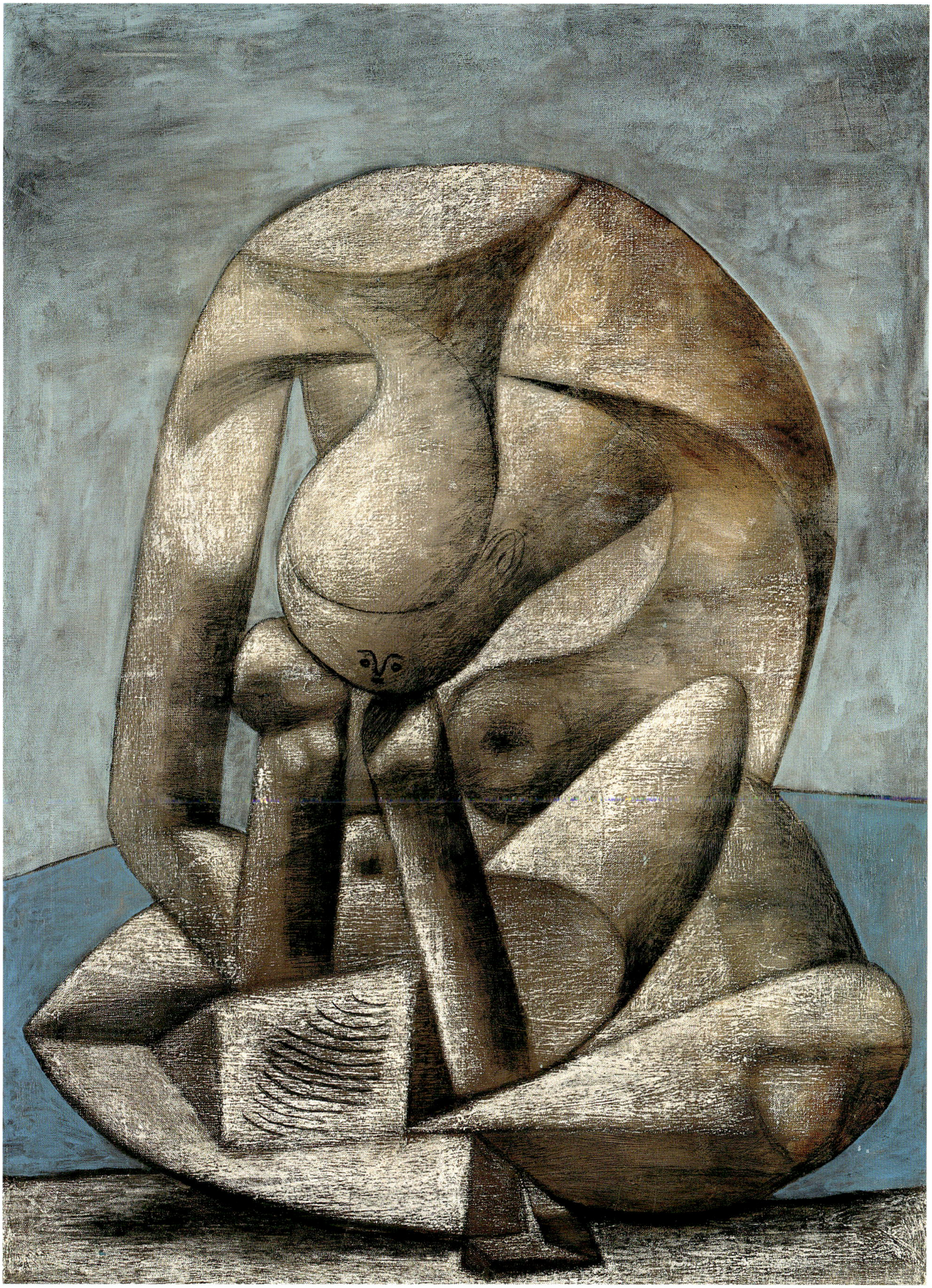

Weeping Woman

18 October 1937, Paris

Oil on canvas

55.3 x 46.3 cm

MP 165

A natural consequence of his desire to express the vast range of human emotions – love, hate, suffering – in painting was Picasso's fondness for depicting women weeping. The emergence of this theme, with which he was obsessed during the autumn of 1937 and which he expressed in various manners – drawings, engravings, painting and sculpture –, coincided with a dramatic period both in his private life and contemporary politics. Derived from *Guernica* (1937, Madrid, Museo Reina Sofia), *Weeping Woman* was in fact the symbol of Spanish women's distress during the Civil War. Her face is a place of horror being torn part like Spain, the painter's native land. But at the same time, it is the face of Dora Maar, the woman Picasso loved who, in his eyes, was the epitome of a woman in tears. Her fiery temperament "inclined to storms and outbursts",[1] according to Brassaï, and the violence of their passionate relationship, observed by biographers, may have given rise to this interpretation, but deeper links testify to this association between Dora and Spain. In fact, Picasso saw her as a politicized companion at one with his art and the problems that haunted him.

The woman's grey face, as dark as soil, stands out in relief against a hastily painted mauve background, her features carved like furrows into the thickness of the paint. The large pointed triangle of the handkerchief, like a threatening object that creates a white hole in the composition, and the green and yellow highlights on the nose and hands accentuate this vision of despair and sadness. The drawing of the facial features is simplified, with just a few lines and crosses indicating the tear-shaped eyes, the twisted mouth and the crevice etched down her cheek.

1. Brassaï, *Conversations avec Picasso*, Paris, Gallimard, 1964, p. 56.

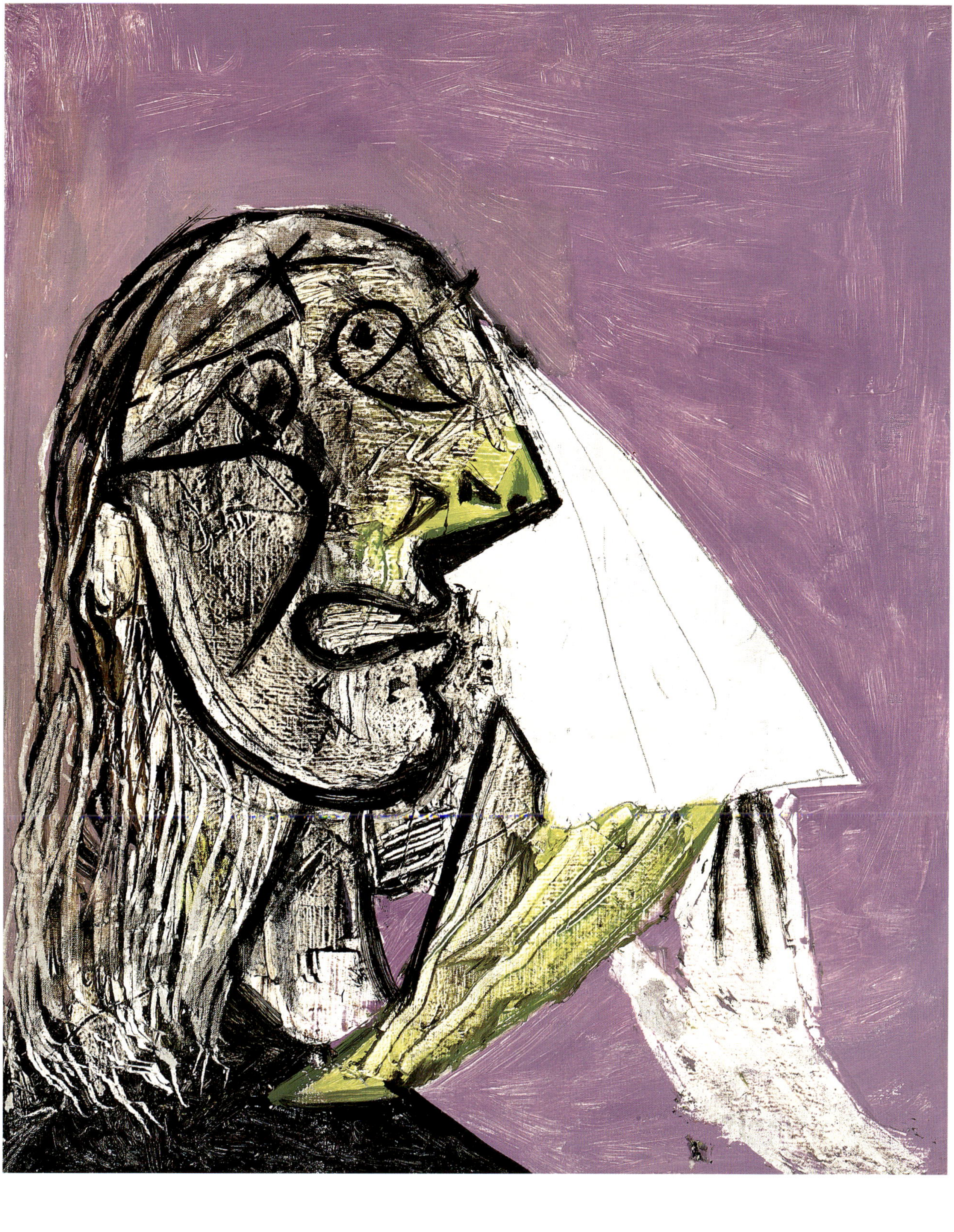

Women at their Toilette

1938, Paris
Pasted wallpaper and gouache on paper mounted on canvas
299 x 449 cm
MP 176

This large collage, made entirely out of pieces of flowery or patterned wallpaper, cut out and pasted onto beige paper, then mounted on canvas, was originally a cartoon for a tapestry for Marie Cuttoli. Although designed in 1938, it was not woven until 1967. This vast cartoon was executed in Picasso's studio in the Rue des Grands-Augustins, and occupied the same place as *Guernica* (1937, Madrid, Museo Reina Sofia).

What was to serve as a model for a wall hanging was made out of paper that usually adorned walls. This particular collage technique, specially adapted to a specific medium, differs from that of the Cubist *papiers collés* in that the cut-out form is the form that is depicted. Picasso paints by cutting out pieces of coloured paper, thereby heralding Henri Matisse's gouaches. The brick-patterned wallpapers are used to suggest the background, the ones with an imitation wood pattern are used for the picture frame and the floor, the floral patterns for the bouquets of flowers, etc. Some of these wallpapers had already been used in the composition of *Guernica*.

The scene represented is a theme dear to Picasso which was famous as early as 1906 – that of a woman having her hair arranged. One woman stands combing the hair of a seated woman, who is looking at herself in a mirror held by a third woman. The presence of the three woman (Dora, Marie-Thérèse, Olga) dates the picture to 1938; the maps of the world adorning one of the wallpapers suggest that this interior scene may have a deeper, allegorical significance.

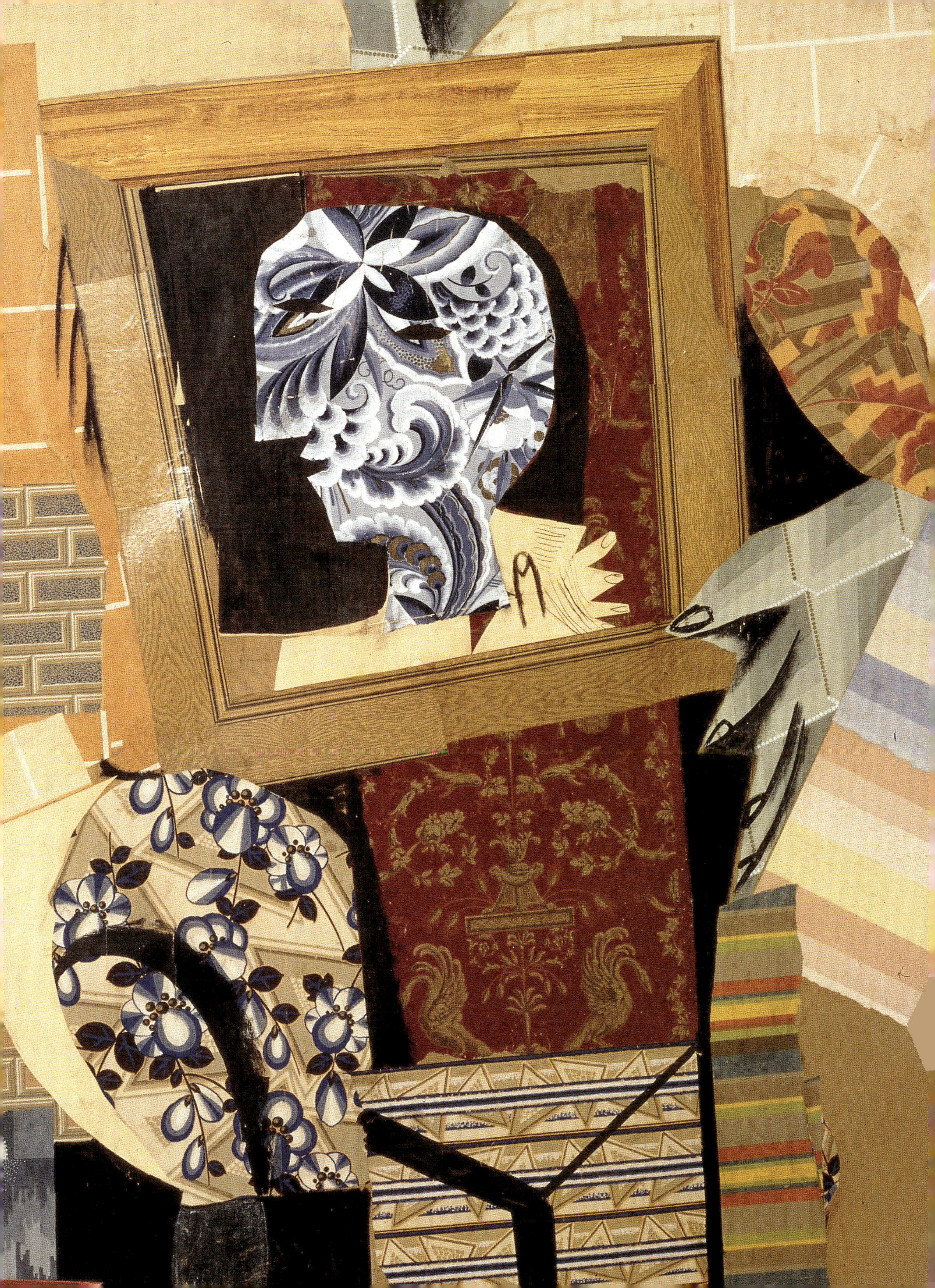

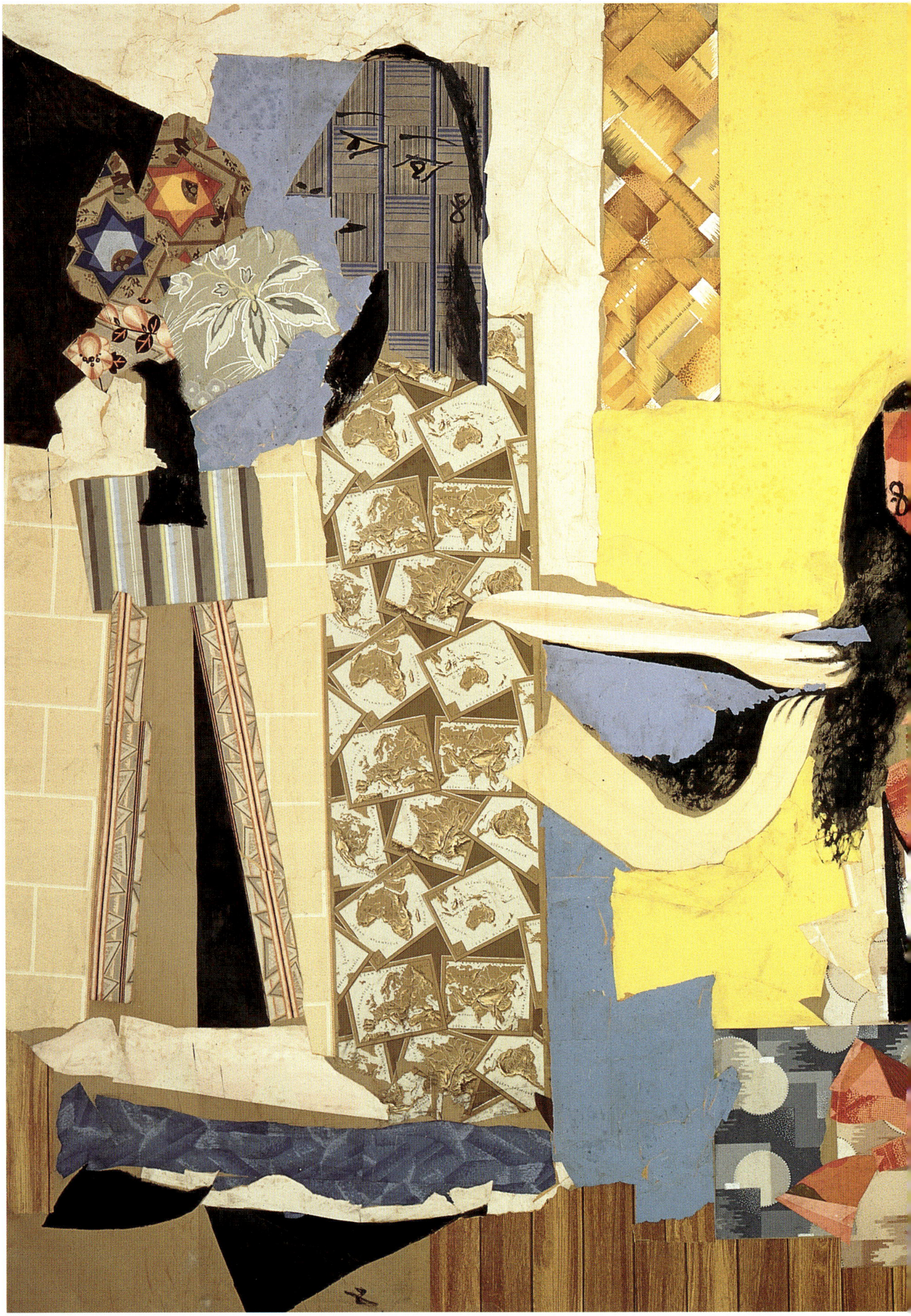

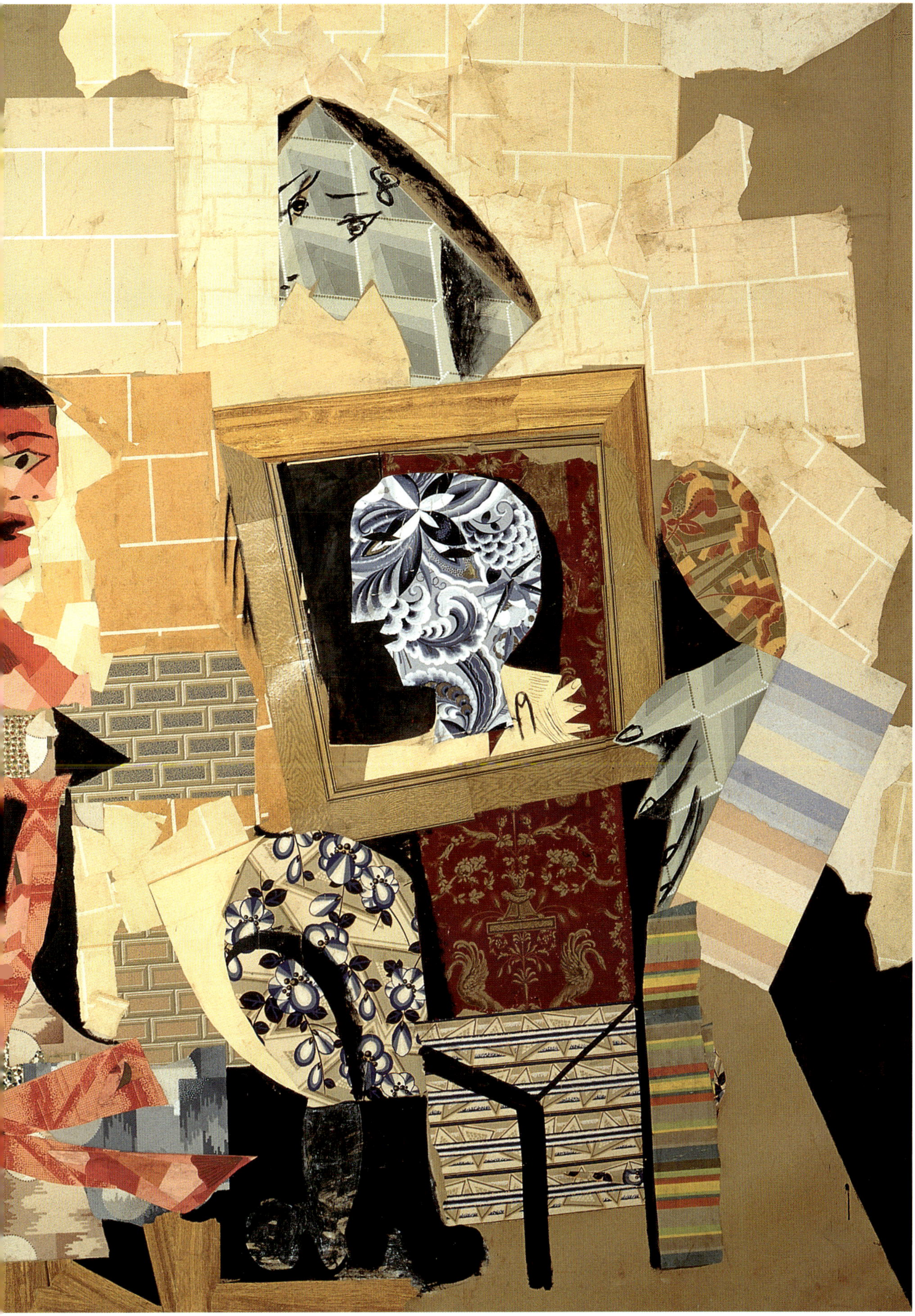

Bust of a Woman with a Striped Hat

3 June 1939, Paris
Oil on canvas
81 x 54 cm
MP 180

In the years 1938-1939, the dislocation of the human face reached its peak. With its menacing looks, faces with proboscis-like appendages or dog's muzzles, wisps of straw and skeins of wool, this series of portraits of huge-headed "Seated Women" or "Women with Hats" is at once the most serious attack on the human face in Picasso's entire oeuvre and his greatest artistic challenge.

How could the expression of the artist's and the era's most complex, most intense feelings merge with the rationality of a formal language, with the coherence of a plastic construction, without moving towards abstraction?

It is the painter's fierce humour, destructive violence and ironic tenderness that transform the woman's face, turn it into a "creature", by endowing it with an individual expression, a character, a specific mood. Here is the great paradox of Picasso's painting and the sign of his genius. In spite of everything, these monsters remain human, because they express the grotesque, monstrous, hidden side of all living beings.

In this painting, the face has assimilated all the graphic motifs around it – the corrugated lines of the straw hat, the vertical stripes of the background, the streaks of the hair. The head is distorted into three distinct, fragmented volumes: a larva-shaped form for the lower part of the face with the mouth and chin, a large canted trapezium for the forehead with lozenge-shaped nose and eye painted in front view, and a flattened oblong for the right profile with an eye as wide open as a window. The head rests on a torso with large, round, white breasts and grey stripes that echo the motifs used on the face. The volumetric treatment of the nose and the simultaneous use of two different viewpoints recall Cubist techniques; the disproportions, inversions and permutations of organs are inherited from the Dinard and Boisgeloup figures; the striped decorative motif, characteristic of this period, is derived from the wicker-basket-cum-heads in the *Dream and Lie of Franco* (series of engravings, 1937).

The realistic pouting mouth affixed to this bizarre form, the staring eyes combined with the pointed nose and long tail of hair, and the ridiculous form of the hat with its green foliage confer an expression of hebetude and stupor upon this figure, who thus becomes disturbing.

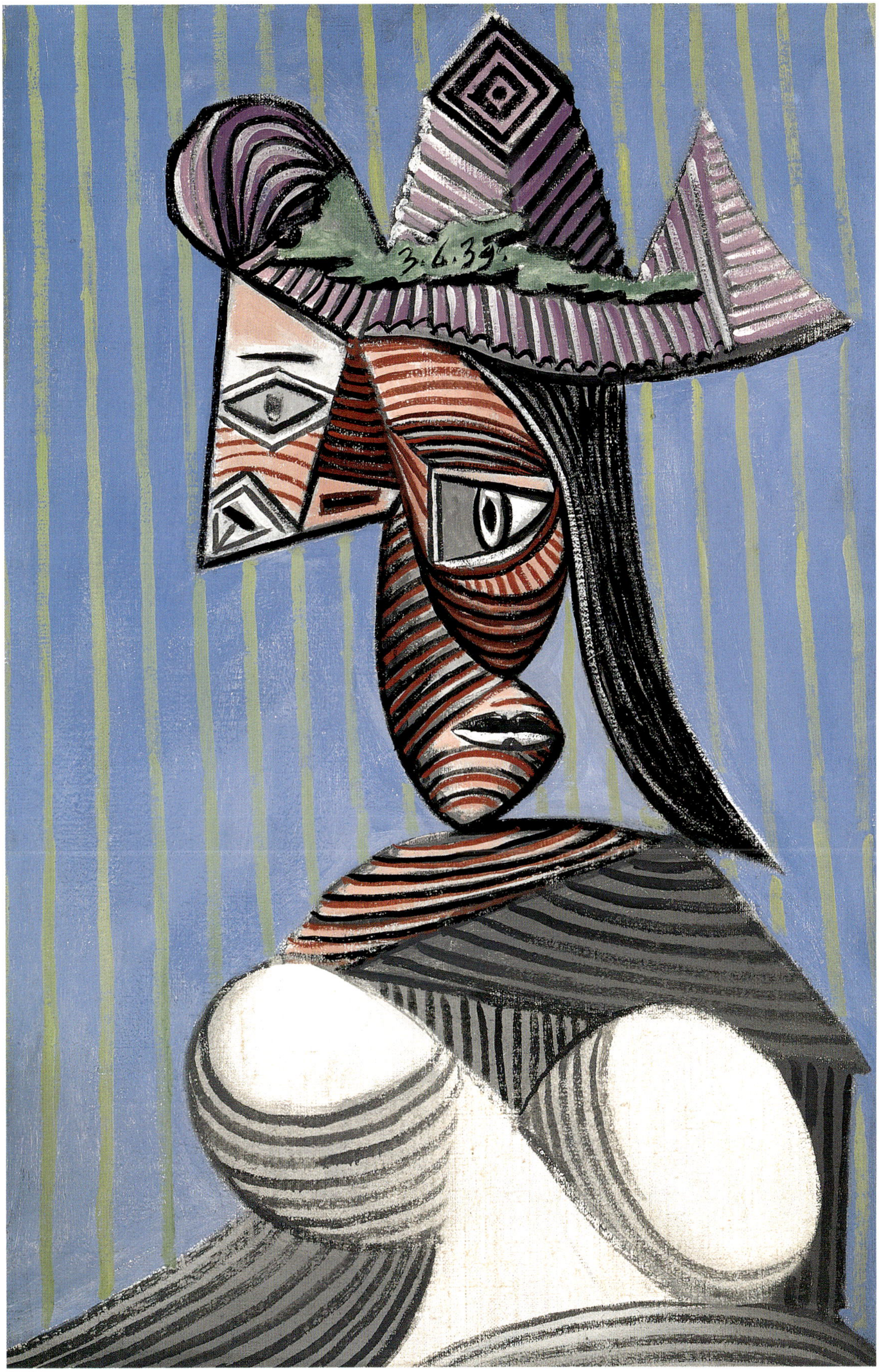
3.6.39.

Boy with a Crayfish

21 June 1941, Paris
Oil on canvas
130 x 97.3 cm
MP 189

In one way or another, all the works executed during the war show the effects of the disquieting, dramatic climate that reigned over the occupied territory at this time. Catastrophes, grief, carnage, torture: all these aberrations of peoples at war which destroy human values have found their pictorial equivalent in Picasso's painting. His monstrous figures, his disintegrated, deformed, grotesque or absurd faces mirror what he feels about the horrors of war. Children do not escape the murderous game played out on his canvases at this time, and it is a theme that recurs on several occasions during this period. More than any other figure, in fact, the child is a combination of monstruosity and innocence, cruelty and silliness, clumsiness and arrogance, victim and tyrant.

And yet, the hope of life to come, this child-king is seated majestically, showing off his penis and brandishing his crayfish like a sceptre. This bawdy little gnome with half his teeth missing, a worthy descendant of Diego Velázquez's dwarfs or Bartolomé Murillo's *Bobo*, epitomizes Picasso's plastic and thematic preoccupations at this time. The seafood – blue fish, octopus and crayfish – is a souvenir from Royan, where the artist spent the first year of the war; however, the child is neither on the beach nor seated at a table: his incongruous position with his penis pointed at the plate like a cannon adds a note of sarcastic humour to the scene. The theme of food is one of the leitmotivs of this period, marked by the daily dread of rationing. The dull, washed-out, greyish green and beige tones are in tune with the pervasive atmosphere of sadness overshadowing the country. The visible brushstrokes announce the vehement style of the late period.

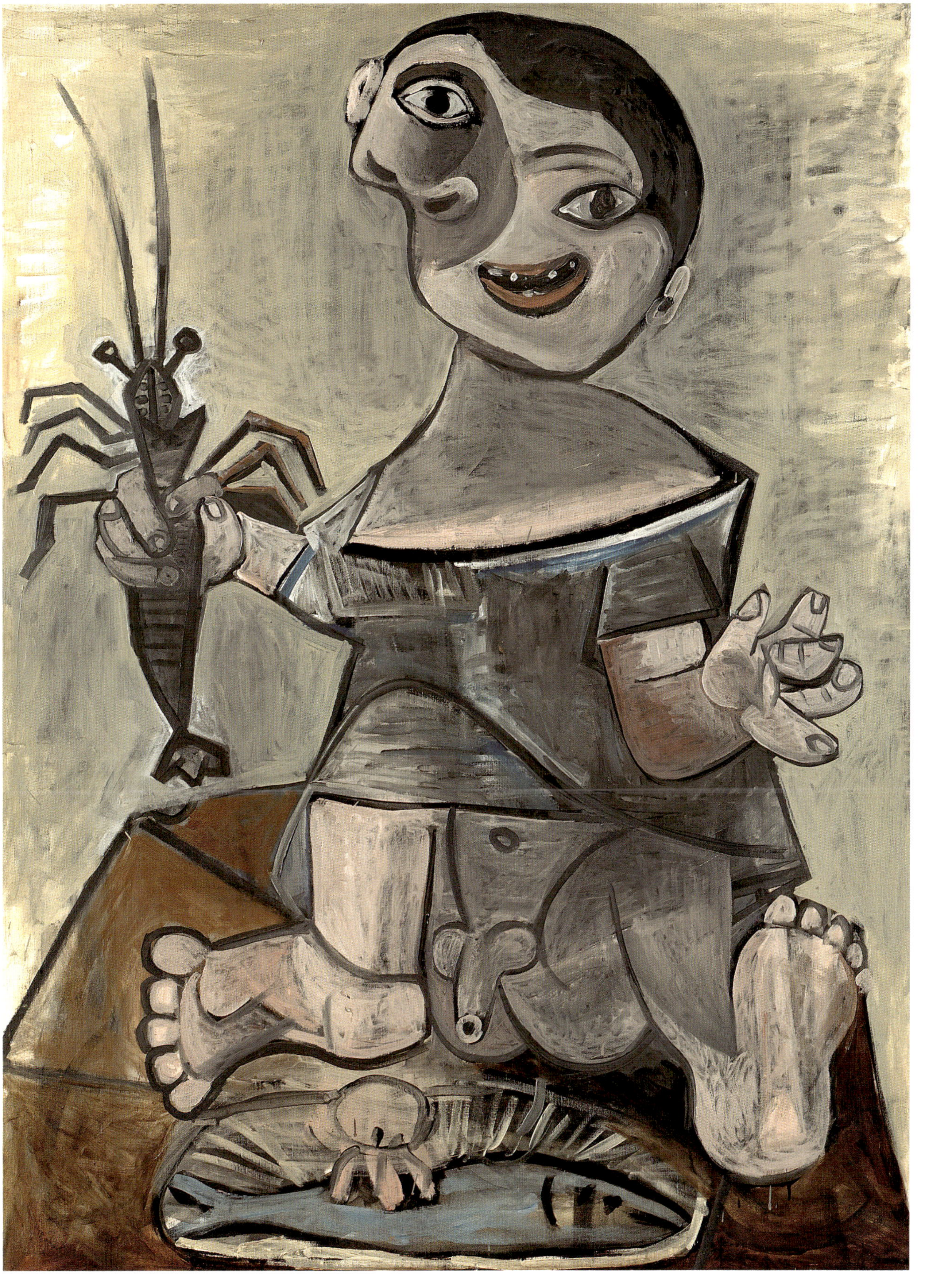

Head of a Bull

Spring 1942, Paris
Leather saddle and metal handlebars
33.5 x 43.5 x 19 cm
MP 330

One of Picasso's most famous sculptures, the *Head of a Bull* assemblage, epitomizes the artist's inventive genius and the special relationship that existed between familiar objects and his prodigious creative spirit. Strictly speaking, the work comprises both the created form and the idea that inspired it, i.e. it is an association of two found objects – a bicycle saddle and a pair of handlebars. This type of work, the fruit of Picasso's skill as a handyman and his fondness for transforming discarded objects, testifies to his exceptionally keen vision of things and to the power of his imagination. Not only did he keep everything he found that he thought might be useful, but at the same time, he saw something else and sensed the underlying formal implications of each object and how he would eventually employ it. It is a pair of handlebars, but also a pair of horns; it is a saddle, but also shaped like a head. If the sculpture is immediately identified as the head of a bull, it is because Picasso instinctively recognized the fundamental schema, the universal archetype, which, from the cave paintings of Lascaux to a child's drawing, represents the bull.

He even wanted to take the paradox further and turn his bull's head back into a saddle and handlebars.

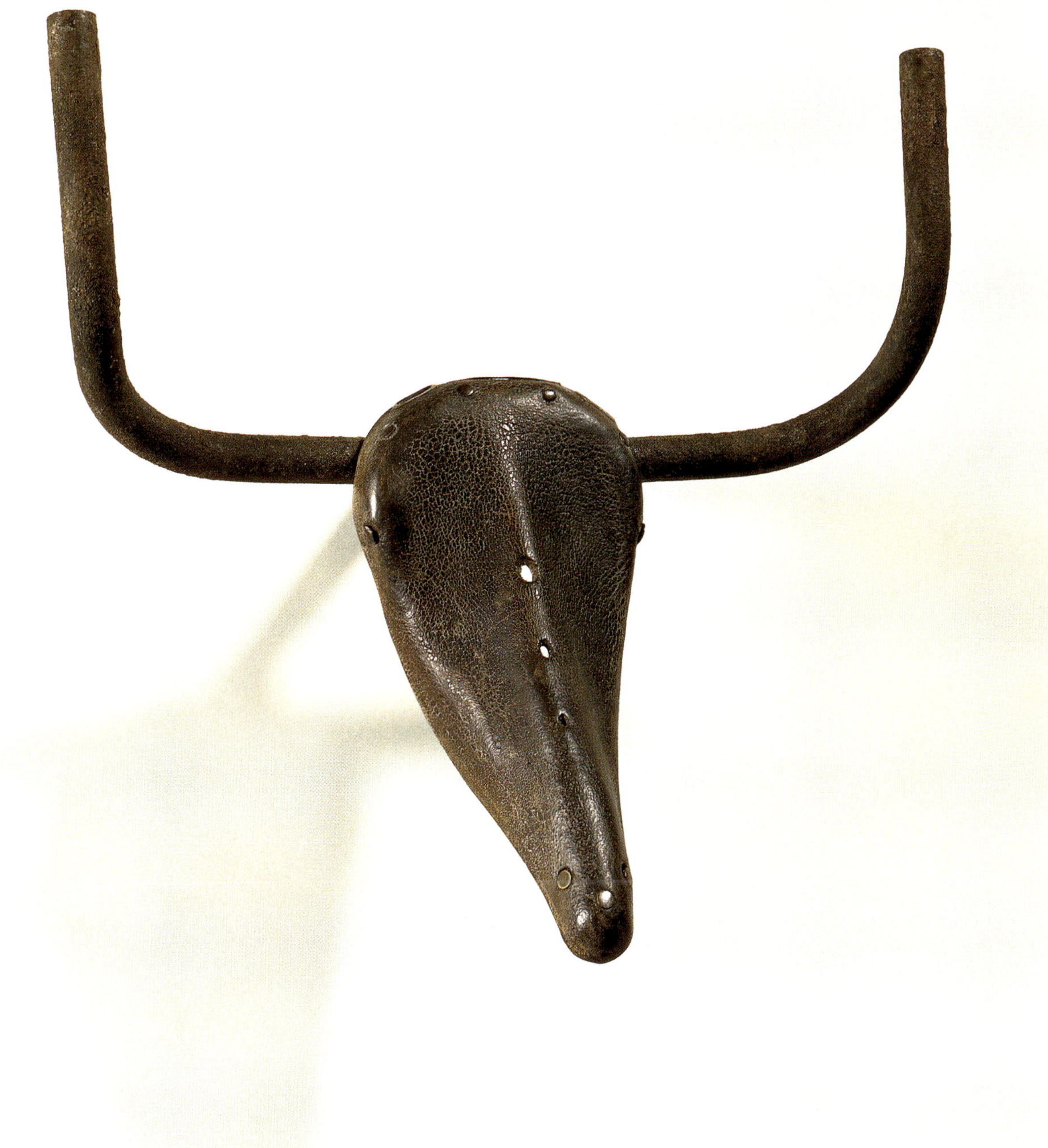

The Kitchen

November 1948, Paris

Oil on canvas

175 x 252 cm

MP 200

In November 1948, Picasso painted two slightly different versions of *The Kitchen*, a huge, grey-toned, monochrome work verging on abstraction. Françoise Gilot remembers how this work originated: "Pablo made a first version of a large painting he called *The Kitchen*. It was based on the kitchen in the Rue des Grands-Augustins, where we sometimes ate our evening meal. The kitchen was painted white, and in addition to the usual kitchen equipment, there were birdcages. Apart from the birds, the only touches of colour were three Spanish plates on the wall. So, essentially, the kitchen was an empty white cube, with only the birds and the three Spanish plates to stand out from the whiteness. One night Pablo said, 'I'm going to make a canvas out of that – that is, out of nothing.'"[1]

The sparer, more radical, first version is thus reduced to a purely linear schema of spatial organization. Then Picasso felt the need to enrich this rather dry drawing pictorially by adding, in the second version, precise, colorful details such as the leaves of the green plant on the right, the design on the plates and the silhouettes of the birds within the cage. Behind the grid formed by the graphic network of dots and lines, he also added zones of colour, whose arrangement and cut-out effects suggest depth and give the painting more density and relief.

This spatial drawing recalls the wire constructions of 1928. The graphic motif of dots and lines first appeared in the abstract drawings, *Constellations* (Paris, Musée Picasso), in 1924. It also recurred in the illustration Picasso did for Paul Reverdy's *Chant des Morts (Song of the Dead)*, in 1943. This specific language, whose origin some see as a simplified bone form and others believe was influenced by Gallic coins, was the starting point for numerous variations in the 1950s.

1. Françoise Gilot and Carlton Lake, *Vivre avec Picasso*, Paris, Calmann-Lévy, 1965, p. 210.

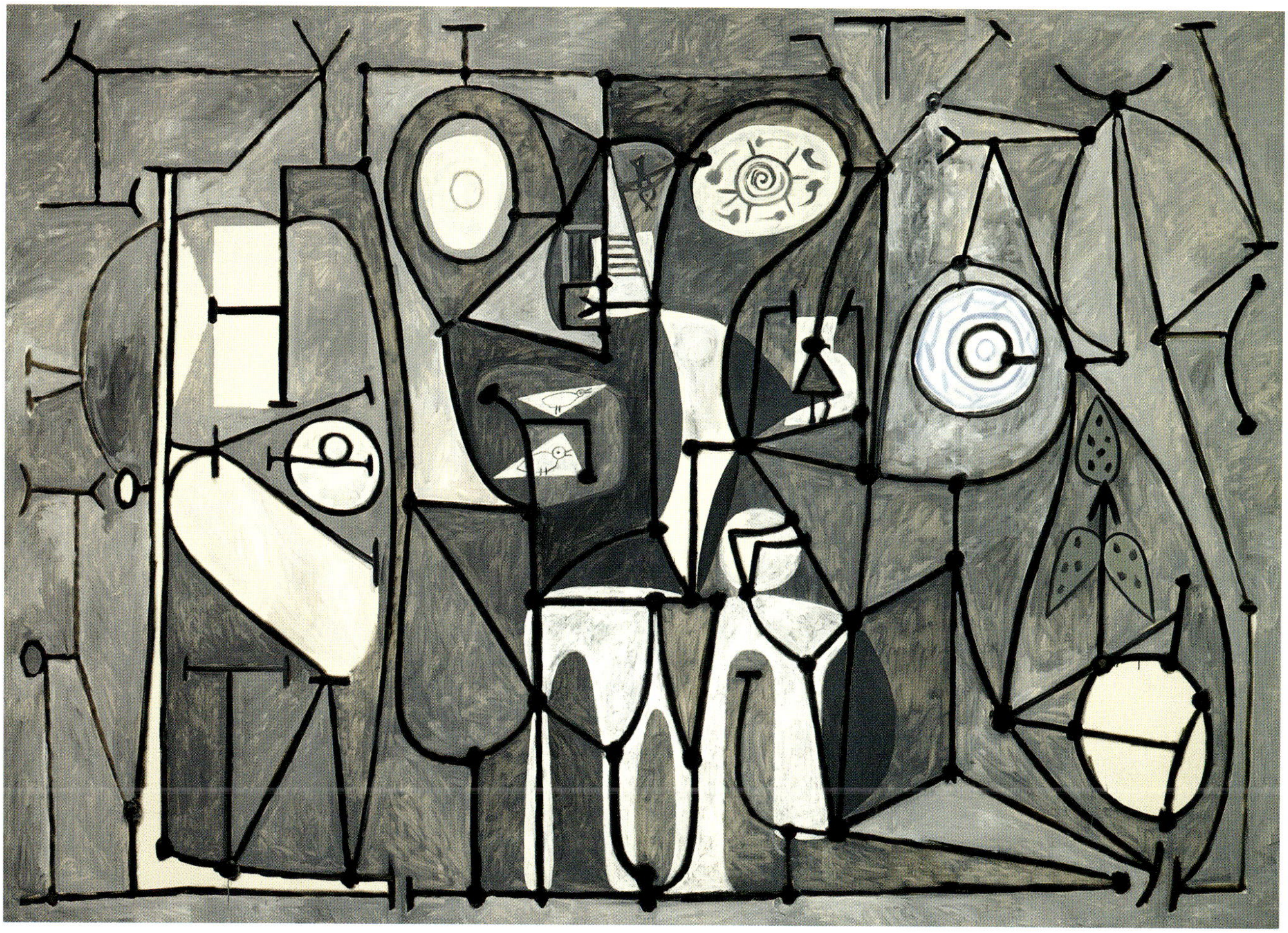

Girl Skipping

1950, Vallauris
Original plaster (wicker basket, cake tins, shoes, wood, metal, ceramics and plaster)
152 x 65 x 66 cm
MP 336

In the same vein as *Woman with a Pushchair* (1950, Paris, Musée Picasso), *Girl Skipping* is a humorous and imaginative combination of modelling and assemblage. With its outstanding technique and subject, this weightless sculpture suspended in mid-air appears as "the sardonic negation of statuary".[1]

"Pablo had always wanted to make a sculpture that didn't touch the ground," relates Françoise Gilot. "One day, while watching a little girl skipping, he found the way to do it. He had the ironmonger in Vallauris make him a rectangular base from which a curved iron tube – in the shape the skipping rope would have as it reached the ground – rose to a height of around a metre. The top ends of this "rope" provided the support for the little girl. The central part of her body was a shallow round wicker basket of the type used to collect orange blossoms for perfume factories. From each side extended a wooden handle, set into the open ends of the metal tube. Pablo attached folds of heavy paper to the bottom of the basket. He poured plaster into these and, when it had dried and he had removed the paper, that made the skirt. Below that, he hung little legs that he had carved out of wood. In the local dump, he had found two large shoes – both for the same foot. He filled them with plaster and attached them to the legs. For the face, he took the round lid of a box of chocolates and filled it with plaster. When the plaster had set, he removed the lid and applied the face to a rectangular plaster form, which had been grooved by pressing it against a piece of corrugated cardboard, one end of which had been trimmed to form the neck. On each side, a slightly curved cutout gave the impression of hair falling down her back."[2]

The originality of these sculpture-assemblages also owes much to the psychological realism expressed in them. Picasso always added anecdotal details to his figures that made them highly expressive: here, the little girl's short skirt, the shoes that are much too big for her, her neatly combed hair and good-as-gold look, while emphasizing her awkwardness and stiffness all help to create the archetypal image of a "little girl". This is a figure whose games, perversity and innocence fascinated Picasso, yet filled him with terror and tenderness, as shown in *The Four Little Girls*, the play he wrote in 1947-1948.

1. André Malraux, *La Tête d'obsidienne*, Paris, Gallimard, 1974, p. 32.
2. Françoise Gilot and Carlton Lake, *Vivre avec Picasso*, Paris, Calmann-Lévy, 1965, p. 290.

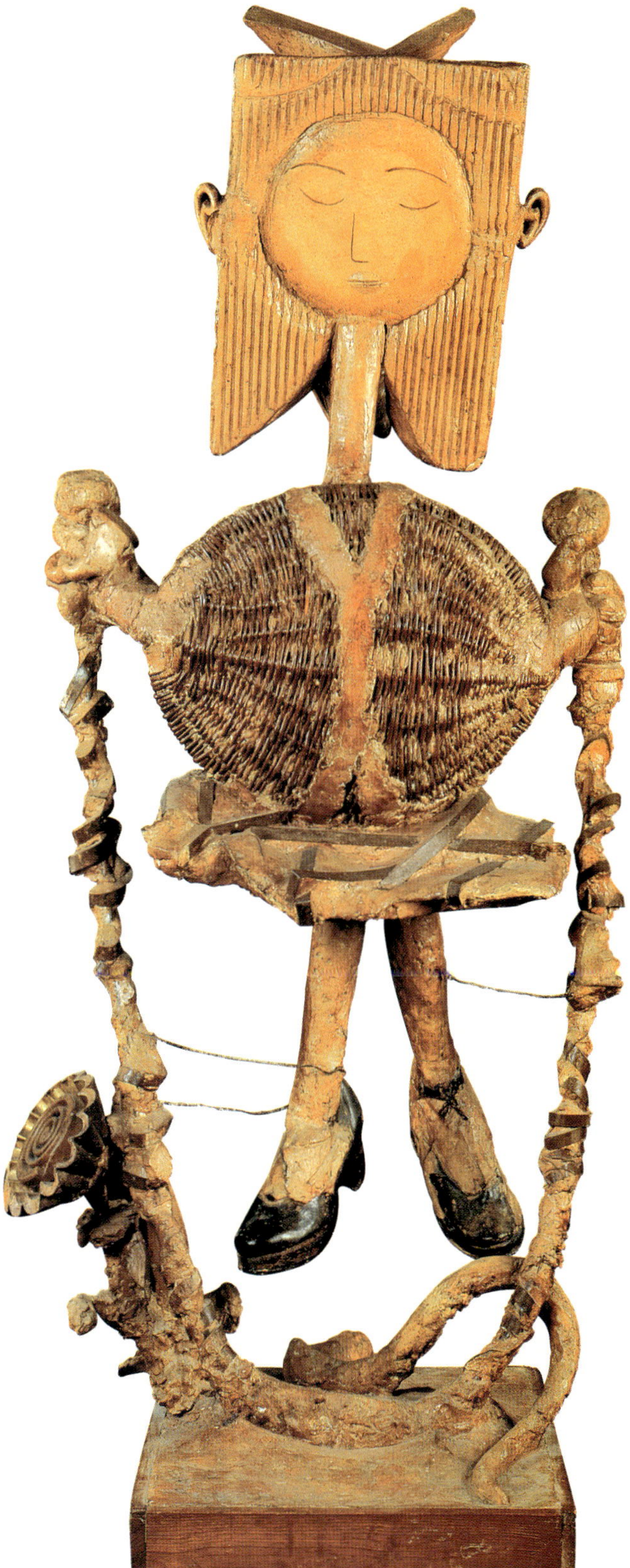

Jacqueline with Hands Crossed

3 June 1954, Vallauris
Oil on canvas
116 x 88.5 cm
MP 1990-26

This famous picture, which marked the entrance of Picasso's last companion, Jacqueline Roque, into his painting, is a companion piece to another portrait, *Jacqueline with Flowers* (private collection), executed the same day, on 3 June 1954. The image of a "modern Sphinx", as she was called by Antonina Vallentin, is indeed evoked by the mysterious look in Jacqueline's almond-shaped eyes, by her long neck and her squatting position. Jacqueline was fond of this pose that would recur in subsequent portraits. It thus prefigured the "Odalisque" series.

When Picasso met Jacqueline, he was struck by her resemblance to the figure smoking a narghile in Eugène Delacroix's *Women of Algiers*. In her, he rediscovered the type of classic, Mediterranean beauty that he had favoured since his stay in Gósol. He would later execute a portrait of her in a black headscarf that turned her into a worthy descendant of the Catalan peasant women of 1906.

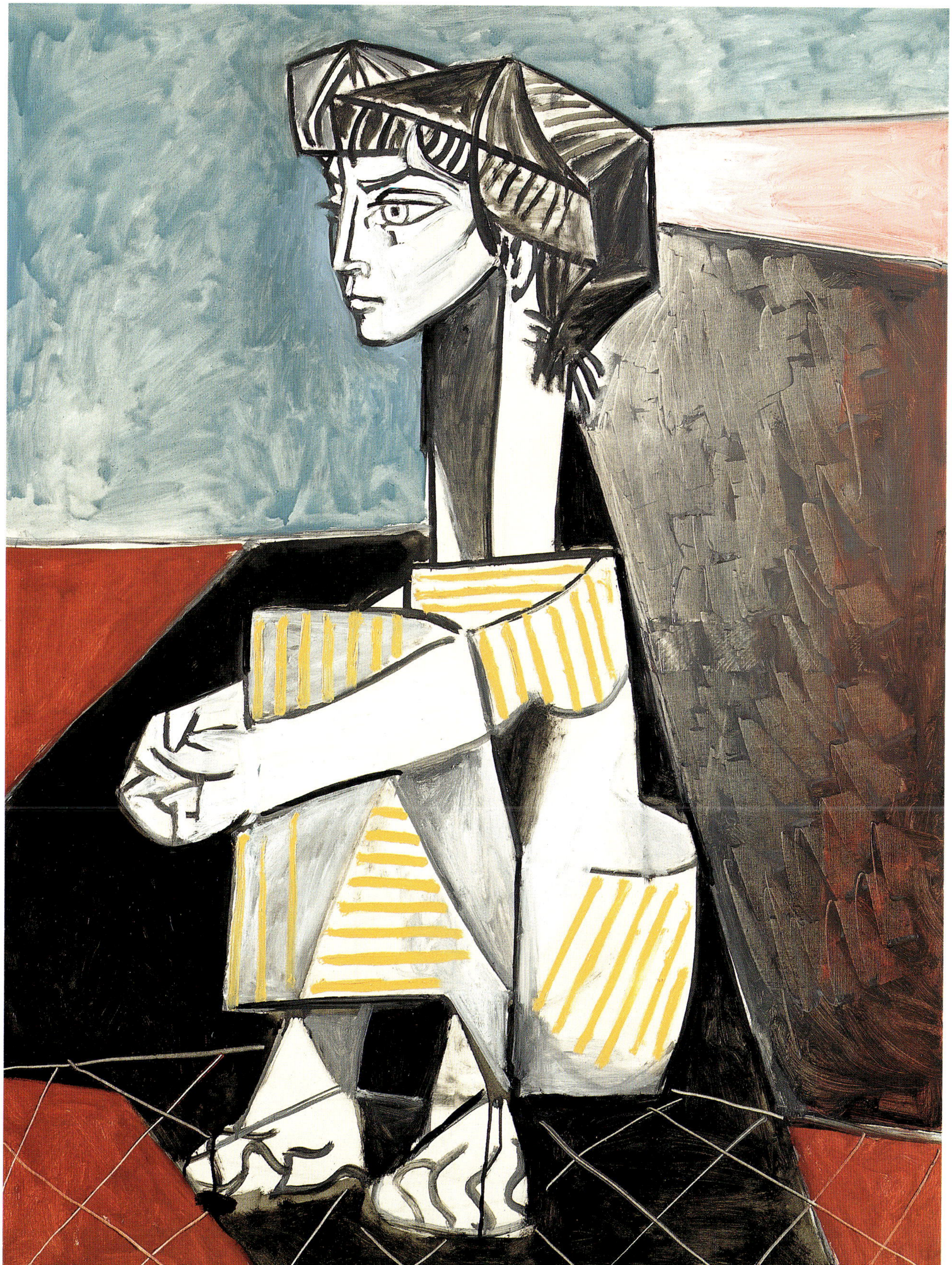

The Bathers

Female Diver
Summer 1956, Cannes
Bronze
264 x 83.5 x 83.5 cm
MP 352

Man with Clasped Hands
Summer 1956, Cannes
Bronze
213.5 x 73 x 36 cm
MP 353

Fountain Man
Summer 1956, Cannes
Bronze
228 x 88 x 77.5 cm
MP 354

Child
Summer 1956, Cannes
Bronze
136 x 67 x 46 cm
MP 355

Woman with Outspread Arms
Summer 1956, Cannes
Bronze
198 x 174 x 46 cm
MP 356

Young Man
Summer 1956, Cannes
Bronze
176 x 65 x 46 cm
MP 357

Picasso revolutionized the art of sculpture in more than one sense. With *The Bathers*, he tackled the problem of compositions with several figures, group sculptures. The six bathers represented here in fact form an inseparable group. From a formal point of view, they are the precursors of flat, geometric sculpture. The figures look like rectilinear posts, whose rhythm is set by the arms and heads, composed of squares, circles, diamonds and diagonals.

The original model was made out of rough planks of wood, nailed together and adjusted to the desired shape. Picasso once again used objects he had found – turned bed legs, broom handles, bits of spade, etc. But here these different elements were cast in bronze; they thus lost their individuality and were used only for their shape and their potential compatibility with the rigid overall structure. This sculpture in geometric bronze plates was the forerunner of the painted sheet metal cutouts of the 1960s, which marked the final stage of Picasso's contribution to 20th-century sculpture.

Despite his use of rigorous forms, which would influence numerous sculptors in the 1960s, Picasso remained faithful to psychological realism, to the expressiveness of the scene portrayed. Each figure has his or her own personality or distinctive character. Picasso could create a living being out of a few pieces of wood nailed together. This skilful use of wood, which had its origins in Cubist constructions, had already been seen in isolated small works, such as *Woman Carrying a Jar* (1935, Paris, Musée Picasso). It would give rise to other works based on the same principle: *Man with a Javelin*, *Head* and *Figure*, three sculptures executed in 1958.[1]

1. Werner Spies, 543, 559, 548.

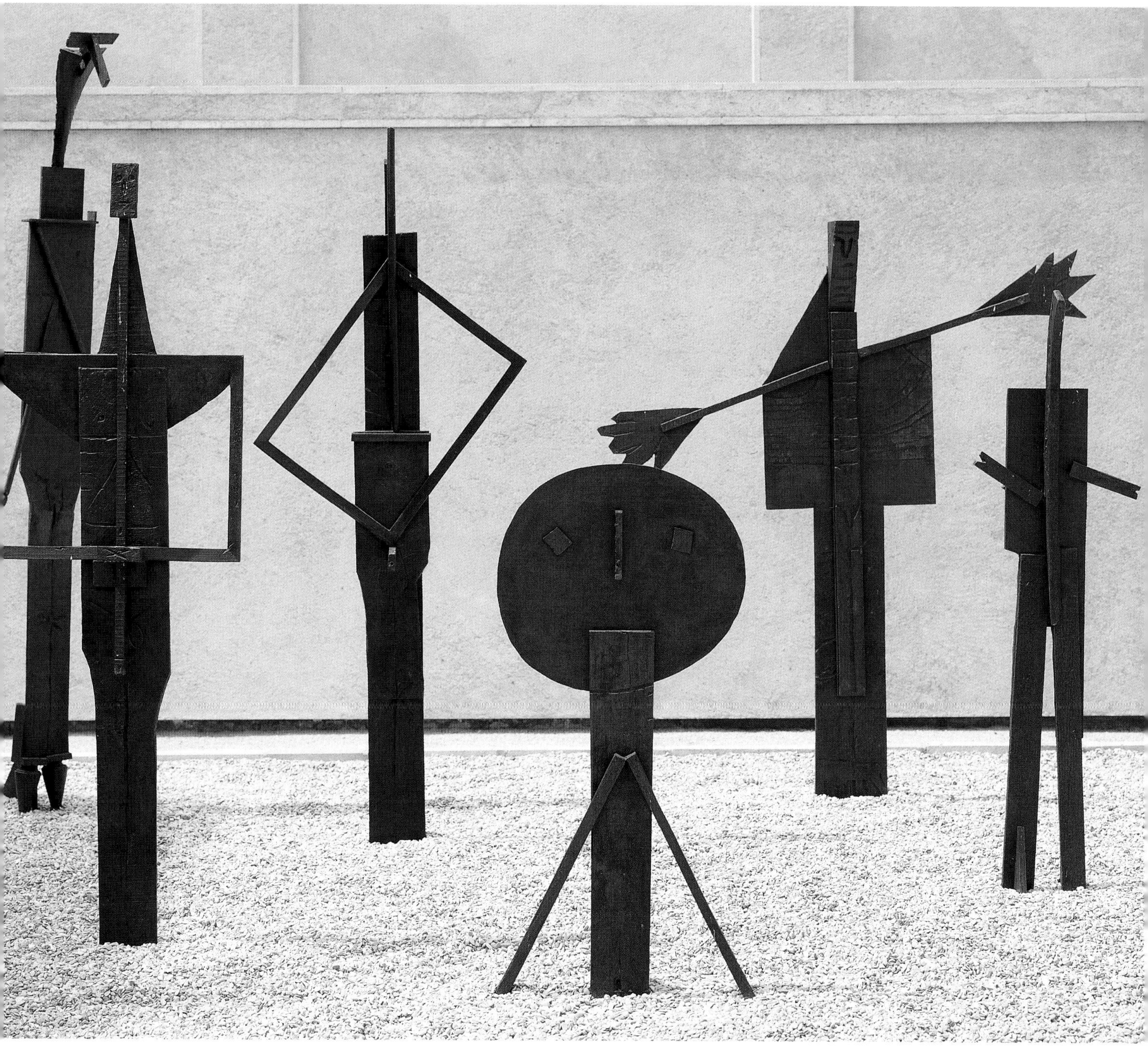

The Studio at "La Californie"

30 March 1956, Cannes

Oil on canvas

114 x 146 cm

MP 211

In 1955, Picasso moved to a new home in Cannes called "La Californie", a spacious, early 20th-century villa, surrounded by a splendid, luxuriant, exotic garden. He converted the vast dining room into a studio, thereby transforming this ornate, baroque universe into a place for painting. The villa's interior design and special atmosphere gave rise to a series of "Studios", which Picasso himself called "interior landscapes", executed between October 1955 and November 1956.

The conventional studio theme, i.e. a painting within a painting, acts as a counterpoint to the "Painter and his Model" series, and may be regarded here as a homage to Henri Matisse, a late response to the studios of 1911-1913 (and also a response to Georges Braque's slightly earlier studios). It is an explicit reference that may be explained by Matisse's recent death, in 1954, and which was already visible in Picasso's *Woman of Algiers* series after Eugène Delacroix, all hymns to colour, Orientalism and his odalisques. Moreover, a recognizable trace still lingers here in the portrait of Jacqueline in Turkish costume, in the bottom right-hand corner of the painting.

The interior decoration of the villa and the objects depicted are easily identifiable: the bronze statue whose triangular form mirrors the form painted on the canvas on the right, the small tabouret with steps, the brown cupboard, the African dish, the painting of Jacqueline in Turkish costume – the only spot of bright colour – and, above all, the Art Nouveau windows, a very plastic motif and the source of endless variations. As in Gustave Courbet's *The Studio*, the centre of the picture is occupied by a canvas, but here it is an untouched, blank canvas, an intoxicating prospect for a painter!

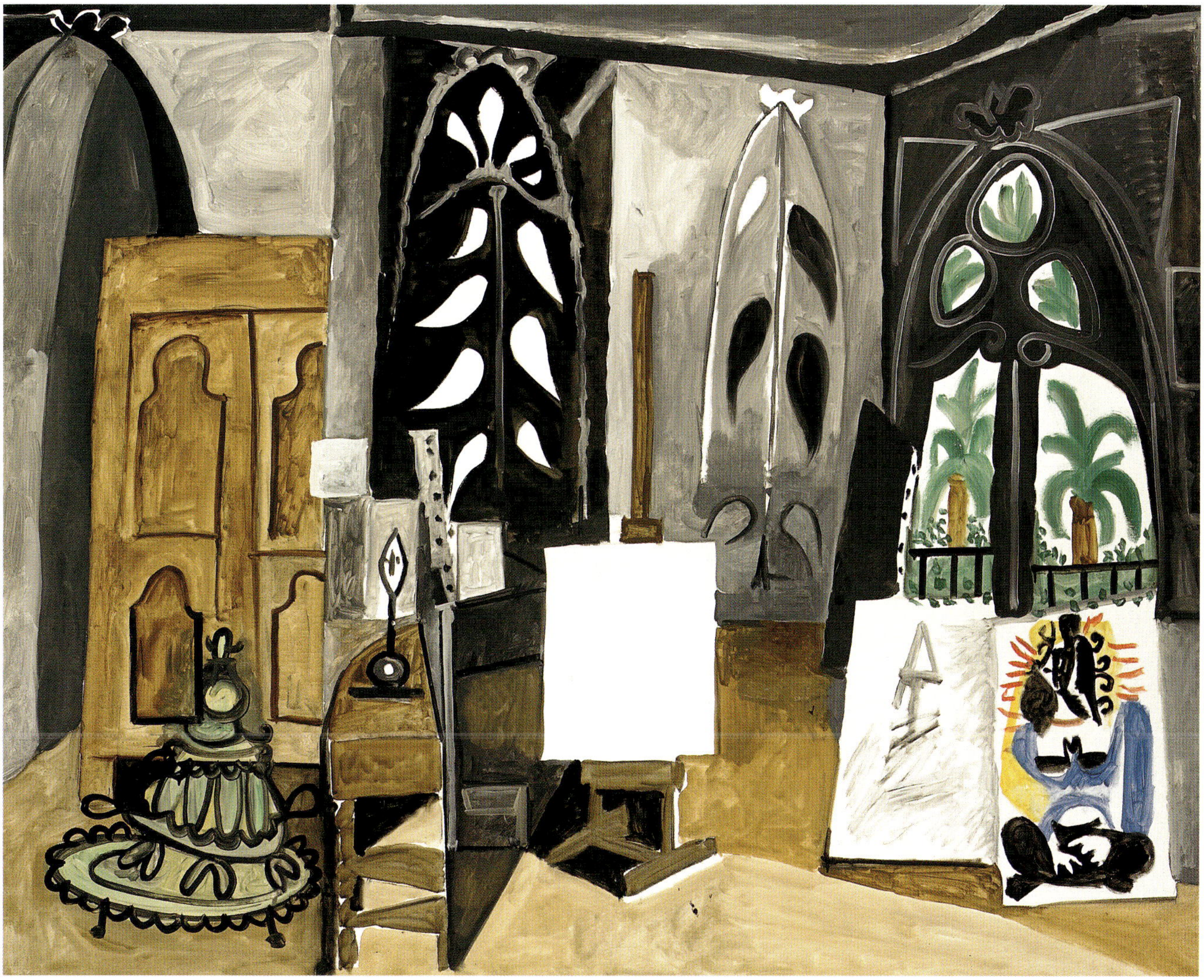

Le Déjeuner sur l'herbe, after Manet

3 March-20 August 1960,
Vauvenargues
Oil on canvas
130 x 195 cm
MP 215

"When I look at Manet's *Le Déjeuner sur l'herbe (Luncheon on the Grass)*, I tell myself, 'hard work for later'," wrote Picasso on the back of an envelope. This short sentence, heavy with meaning and surprising in its premonitory character says much about how deeply Picasso related to Manet, the importance of what was at stake, the intensity and prolificacy of the dialogue. Throughout his life, Picasso is known to have drawn inspiration from past masterpieces. At different stages of his career, he felt the need to confront his predecessors, to borrow a theme, a motif from the dictionary of universal art.

Commenced in August 1959 and completed in July 1962, *Le Déjeuner sur l'herbe* cycle, the last on the theme of interpreting past masters, following the series entitled "*Women of Algiers* after Delacroix" and "*Las Meninas* after Velázquez", was in fact the most prolific, the one that lasted the longest and produced the largest number of variations on the original model. In this version, Picasso respected the figures' positions and the surroundings (trees, clearing, river), as well as the dominant blues, greens and pinks and even details such as the still life in the foreground. But he left out one of the men so as to highlight the relationship between the man who is talking on the right and the monumental, seated woman on the left – a confrontation which brought him back, in spite of himself, to the essential dialogue between the painter and his model, one of Picasso's favourite themes that precedes, accompanies and continues after that of the "*Déjeuners*".

In these stylistic exercises, Picasso in fact added to the work without upsetting the structure completely. Each type of interpretation corresponded to a different style: he adapted his formal language to the situation, as if he wanted to test his own plastic discoveries on a given model. Here, an extremely tight, scalloped technique, which enabled him to insert the figures into a decorative background, and swirling impasto.

What did Picasso find so fascinating about this work that made him explore it so passionately? First, it was a subject that enabled him to tackle landscape. Secondly, the nudes were a response to Paul Cézanne's *Great Bathers* and Henri Matisse's *La Joie de Vivre*. From one, he borrowed the idea of depicting nude figures in a landscape and the architectural solidity of the overall work; from the other, he took the idyllic, pastoral atmosphere.

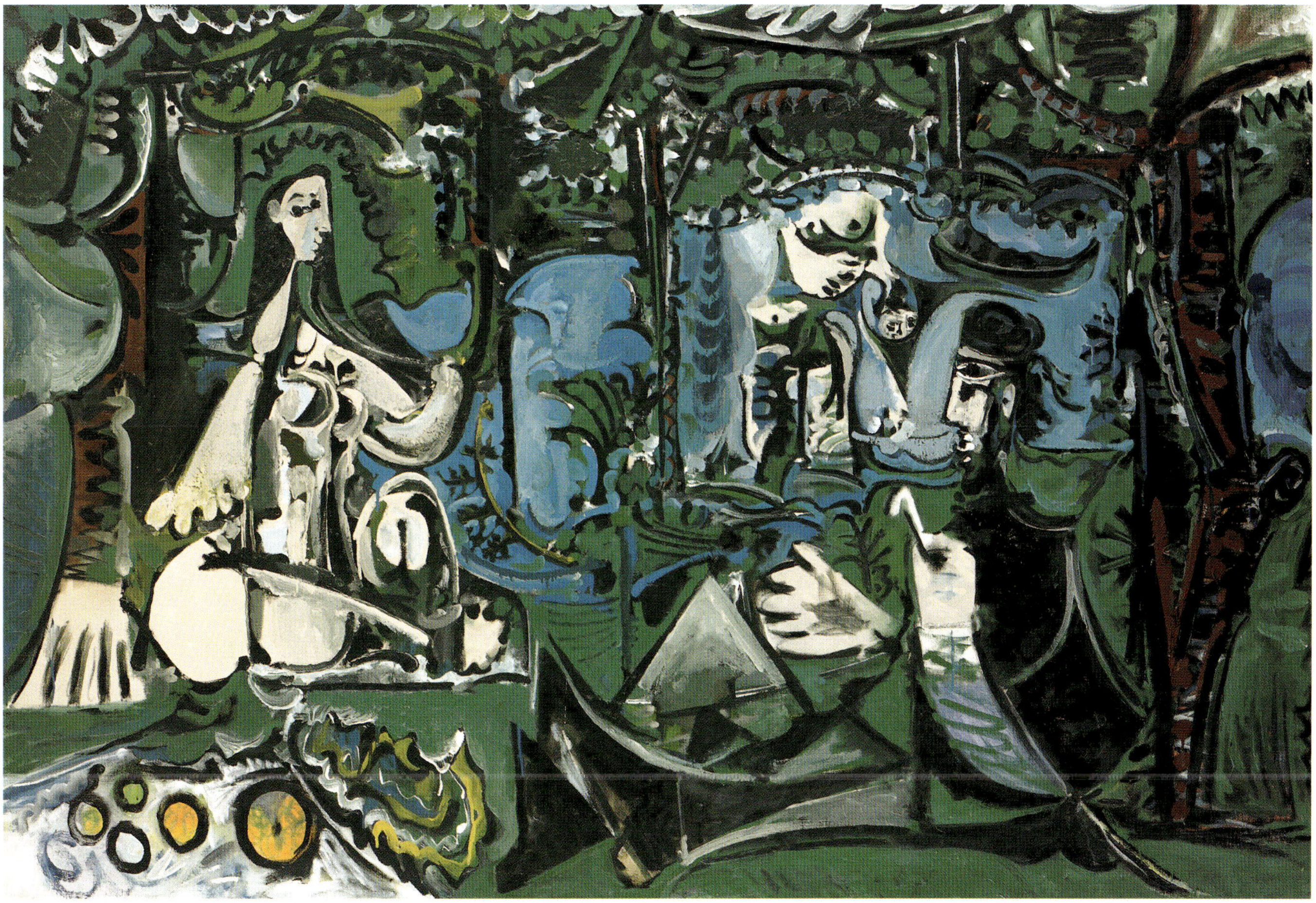

Woman with Pillow

10 July 1969, Mougins

Oil on canvas

194 x 130 cm

MP 1990-35

Parallel to his exploits and bold experiments, Picasso continued to work in what could be termed a "classical" vein, as is demonstrated by this seated nude, painted entirely in black and white. The artist seldom used a palette made up exclusively of greys, ivories and whites. One has to go back to paintings such as *Olga with a Fur Collar* (Lille, Musée des Beaux-Arts) or *The Idyll* (Marina Picasso Collection), both executed in 1923, to find similar tones, although white is not used here to cover the drawing, but is the principal colour in which the picture is actually painted.

Picasso executed several preparatory studies – focusing on the face and this half-seated, half-reclining pose against a lace-edged pillow – for this splendid portrait of Jacqueline that recalls Francisco de Goya's *Maja Desnuda*. The expressiveness of the face stems from the almost natural insertion of the profile into the frontal view. The reclining nude theme had already been explored in 1967, but in a more burlesque manner. The monumental stature of this female body depicted in a frontal view shows to what extent a woman's body lends itself to painting: "Jacqueline has an incredible gift for becoming painting."[1] Since this was one of Jacqueline Picasso's favourite paintings, she bought it back from the Galerie Louise Leiris.

1. Hélène Parmelin, *Picasso dit...* Paris, Gonthier, 1966, p. 80.

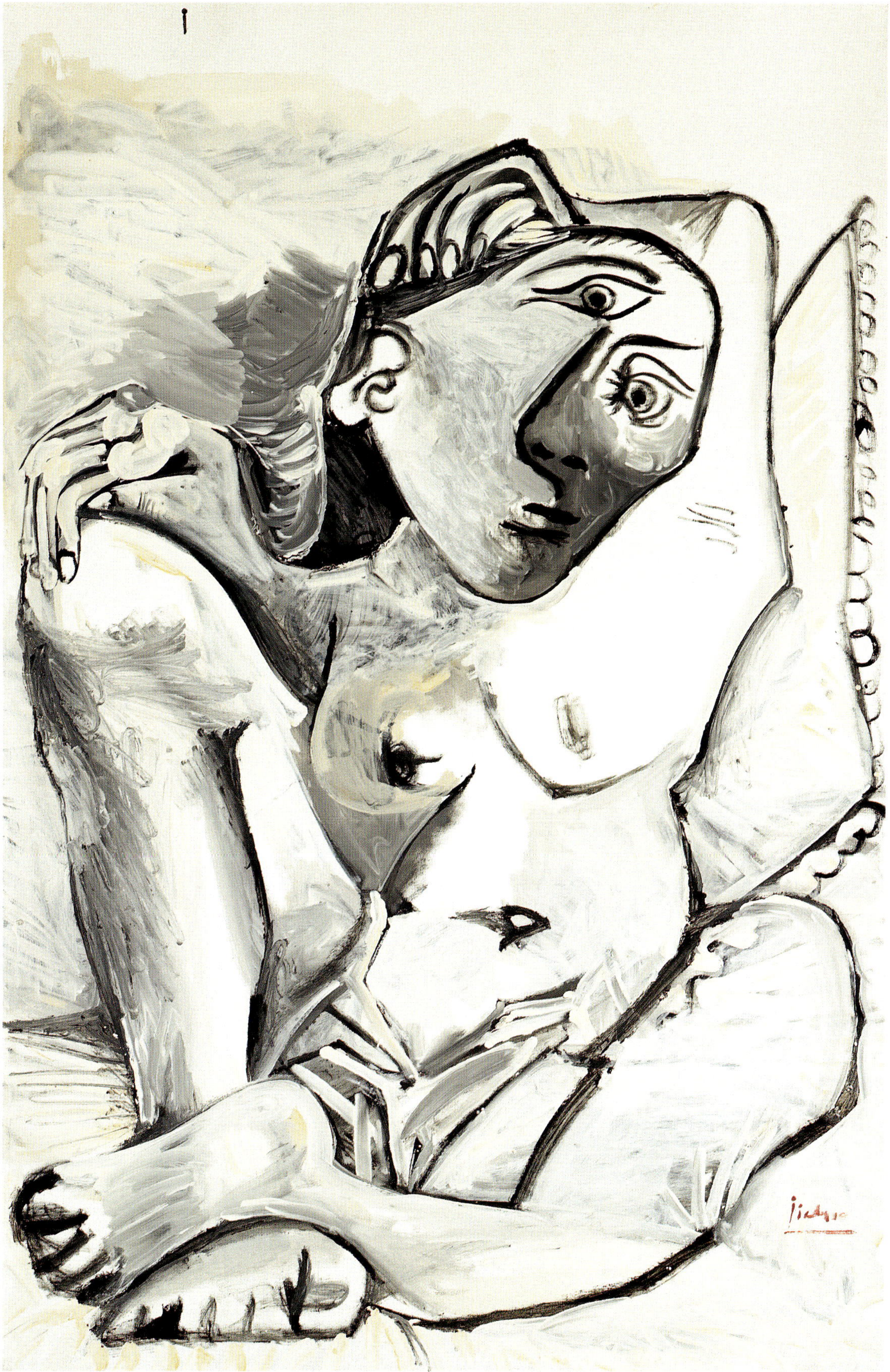

Reclining Nude and Man Playing the Guitar

1970, Mougins
Oil on canvas
130 x 195 cm
MP 224

In this painting, Picasso returns to a theme he had already explored in several variations (*Dawn Serenade*, 1942, Paris, Musée National d'Art Moderne), i.e. that of music and love. The ties between a musician, flute player or guitarist and a naked woman are symbolized by a musical tribute. The guitar is treated here as a calabash gourd, its affinity with the female silhouette confirming the interest Picasso always showed in this instrument; for him, the guitar evoked the *cante jondo* of his Andalusian childhood as well as the contours of a woman's body. The characteristic pictorial technique of the Avignon period can again be be seen in this painting: hastily drawn schematic forms, fundamental graphic motifs such as the backbone of a fish for the genitals, the diagonal stripes for the background, the corkscrew curls of the beard and the enormous, fan-shaped hands and feet. The form of the heads recalls earlier profiles from the Boisgeloup period, with their prominent noses.

The woman's body is twisted so that each part of it is in turn visible and flattened against the picture surface. The paint is applied thickly, is reworked in places, slapped on hastily in others, showing the marks of the brushstrokes. Through a play of transparency and superposition, these "daubing" effects create a subtle range of tones.

"Painting remains to be done," said Picasso towards the end of his life, as if he had to start all over again, as if his painting was still at a very early stage, in an archaic phase, in its infancy.

In fact, after having jeopardized, during the Cubist revolution, the legacy left by the Renaissance, by attacking one of its fundamental precepts – perspective illusionism –, Picasso, the creator of a new picture space, opened up further areas of investigation in painting. And, at the end of this agonizing journey, after having said everything there was to say in every possible way, even assuming, in the late years, the weight of tradition, the legacy from the past, came the final interrogation, the questioning of all he knew: "What is painting, and how should one paint?"

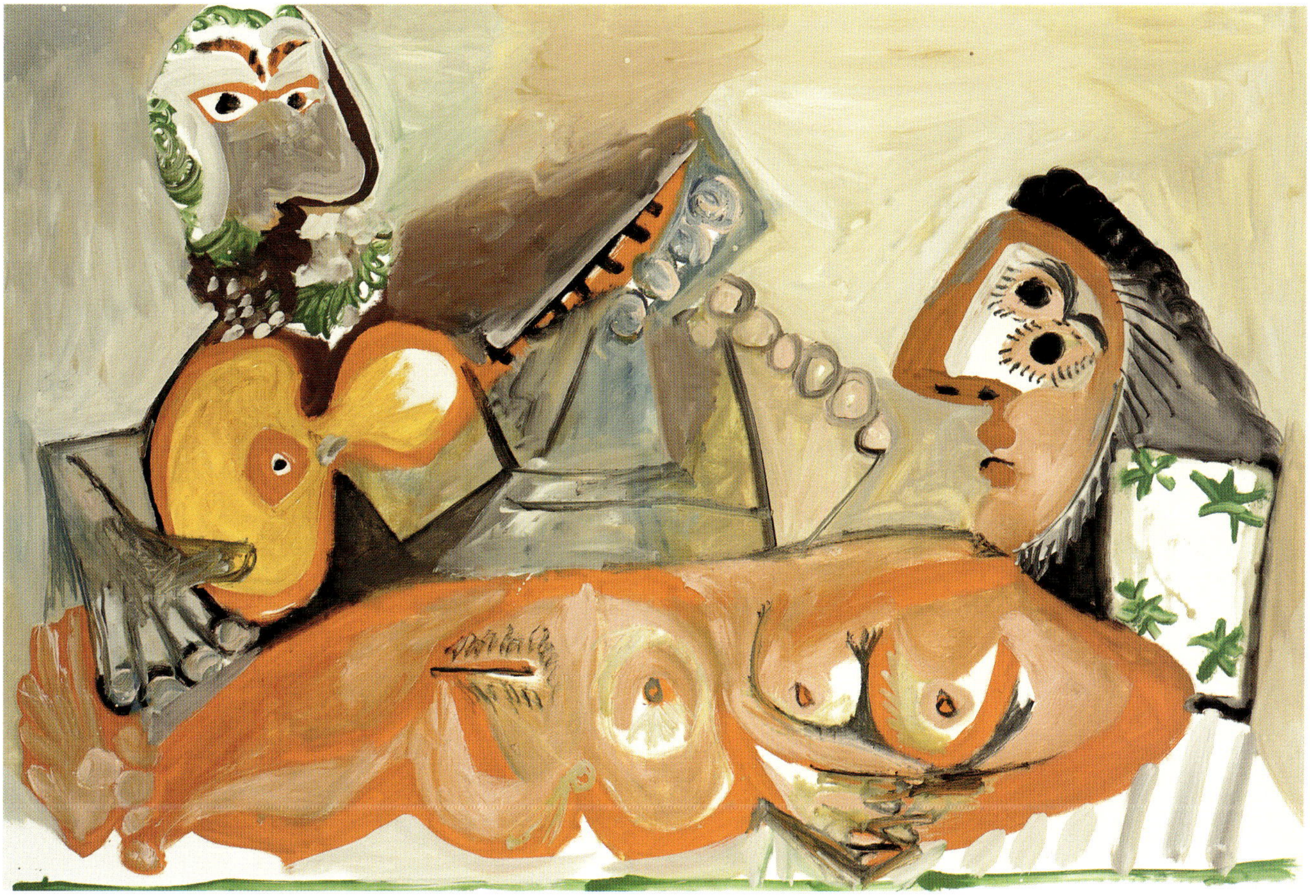

Landscape

31 March 1972, Mougins

Oil on canvas

130 x 162 cm

MP 227

Being more interested in the human figure, Picasso painted few landscapes and those that are known today were seldom pure landscapes. They were more often familiar, nearby views, which he could see from his window and which he portrayed in perspective or in panoramic views.

This canvas dates from March 1972: Picasso was 91 years old and this lively, sketchlike, action painting, characteristic of the late period, said to represent Avignon in memory of his exhibitions at the Papal Palace in 1970 and 1973, testifies to a completely free style – "free figuration", i.e. the recognition of painting as an independent, living medium that creates its own symbols. The handling plays on impasto, trickles, visible brushstrokes and the transparency of superimposed layers of paint. The writing is very assertive – dots, black and white spots, corkscrew motifs, thick stripes, in zigzags or radiating out from the centre, fishbone, vertical lines topped by circles, and a diagonal arrow. All these symbols fit into one another, creating a broad grid, suggesting the lines of force that structure the composition, control the dense medium and add a dramatic aspect to this action painting. A dramatic effect that is heightened by the work's overall glaucous, greenish, opacified tones. These motifs are like ideograms and recur in other paintings – the fishbone can be found in *The Musician* (1970, Paris, Musée Picasso) and represents the female genitals in several drawings; the arrow and the circular motifs are also sexual symbols.

Picasso handled nature like a living organism, infusing it, as he did his bouquets of flowers and women's bodies, with a raw, primitive, elementary vitality. In his old age, the accomplished example he set was that of a return to the infancy of art.

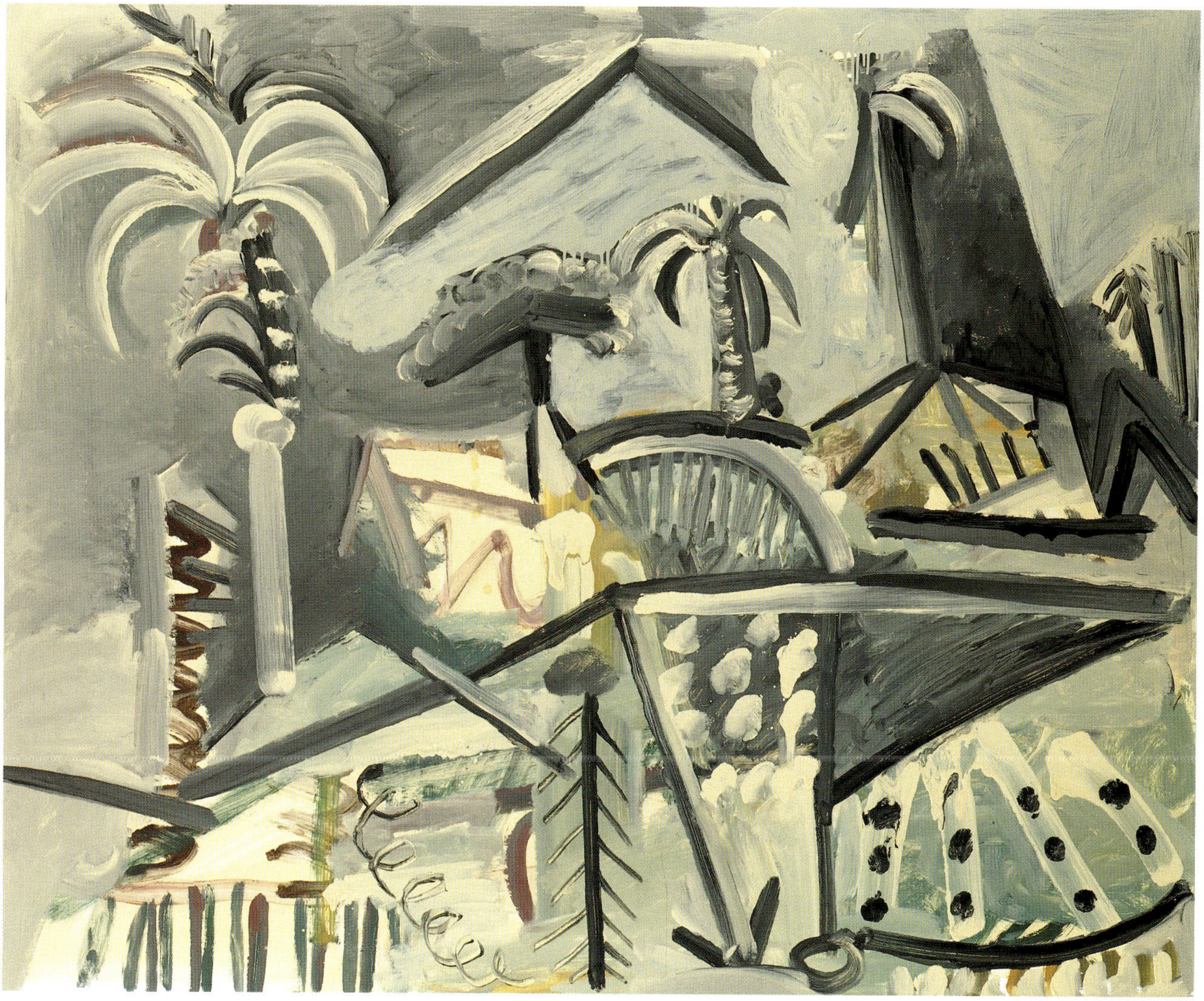

Seated Old Man

1970-1971, Mougins

Oil on canvas

145.5 x 114 cm

MP 221

"Nothing can be done in solitude. I have created a solitude for myself that nobody suspects."

Pablo Picasso to E. Tériade, 1932

A fateful portrait of the elderly painter, this flamboyant painting, which condenses several pictorial, formal and symbolic references in a single image, represents, in fact, the most moving and the most tragic of Picasso's self-portraits. Not only a portrait of the artist at the end of his life, but also of Matisse, Van Gogh, Renoir and Cézanne, all reunited here to express the drama of man's approaching death, the despondency of knowledge, the weight of existence, solitude, nostalgia and the mortal fatigue of a gaze that has seen everything and that, at the last minute, remembers essential images, violent passion and lastly painting, to which one sacrificed his ear and the other his hand. But Picasso remains Picasso, and the vital force that vivified him transforms old age here into an apotheosis, as is shown by the vigorous brushwork, the swirling, Fauve-like colours, and the squiggles and trickles of paint.

The reference to Henri Matisse is the most evident: a drawing dated 1971 representing a bearded old man wearing a hat with the inscription "a bit like Matisse", the warm contrast between the bright orange and cobalt blue, and the allusion to his *Romanian Blouse* hidden in the curve of the armchair are all indications that this work was a final tribute to "the old white, bearded god" (Picasso). The straw hat – one of the artist's attributes together with the palette – was borrowed from Van Gogh's self-portraits. The obscene stump of the hand is probably a reference to the paralyzed fingers of the elderly Auguste Renoir, whose photograph Picasso kept and used to make a drawing. Mutilation seems to be the key to this painting: the fear of death, the dread of being incapable of painting which was once conveyed by blindness, and is expressed here by the amputated limb. "... through it Picasso forever holds the terrible pose of *The Man with a Hand Cut Off*."[1]

1. Jean-Michel Michelena, *Vieil homme au chapeau assis*, Bordeaux, Cape, 1983.

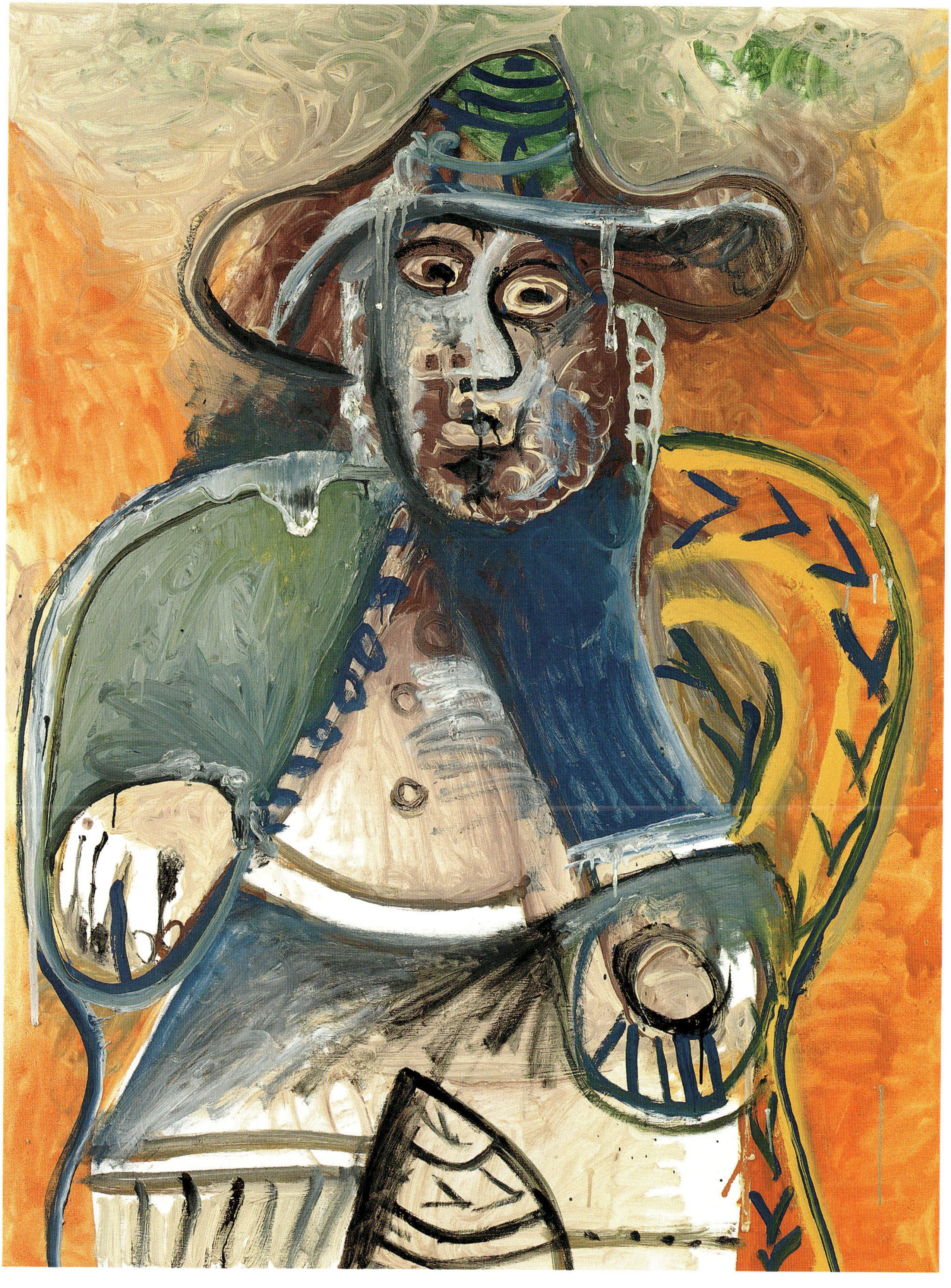

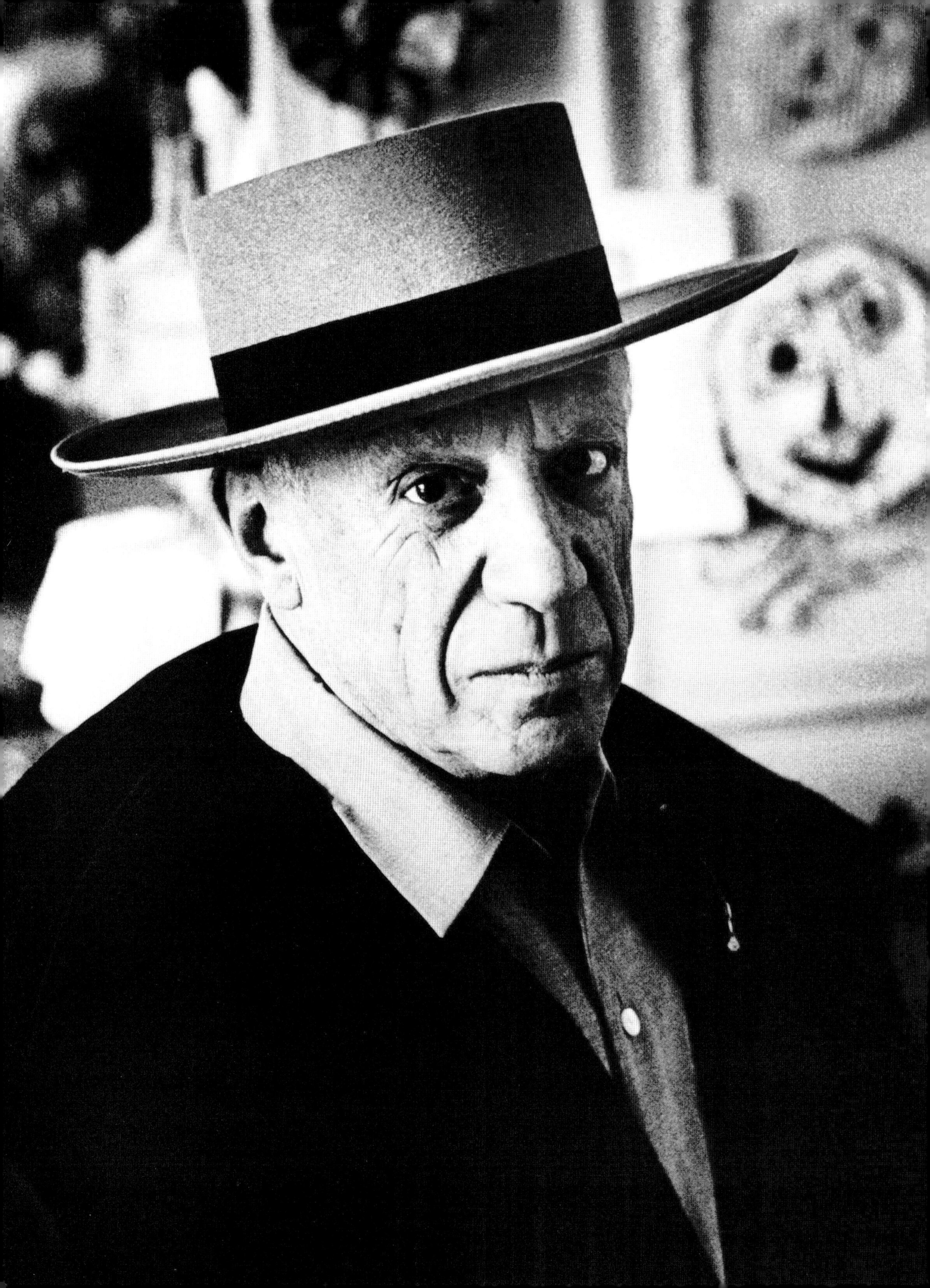

Biography

David Douglas Duncan
Portrait of Picasso with Hat
1957-1958

1881 25 October: Pablo Picasso born in Málaga, Spain, the son of Don José Ruiz Blasco and Maria Picasso y López, originally from Genoa.

1891 In September, the Ruiz family arrive in La Coruña.

1895 Picasso attends La Lonja, the Barcelona School of Fine Arts, where his father is a professor.

1897 Picasso is admitted to the San Fernando Academy, Madrid.

Picasso and his sister Lola (after an original print)
Malaga
c. 1886-1887

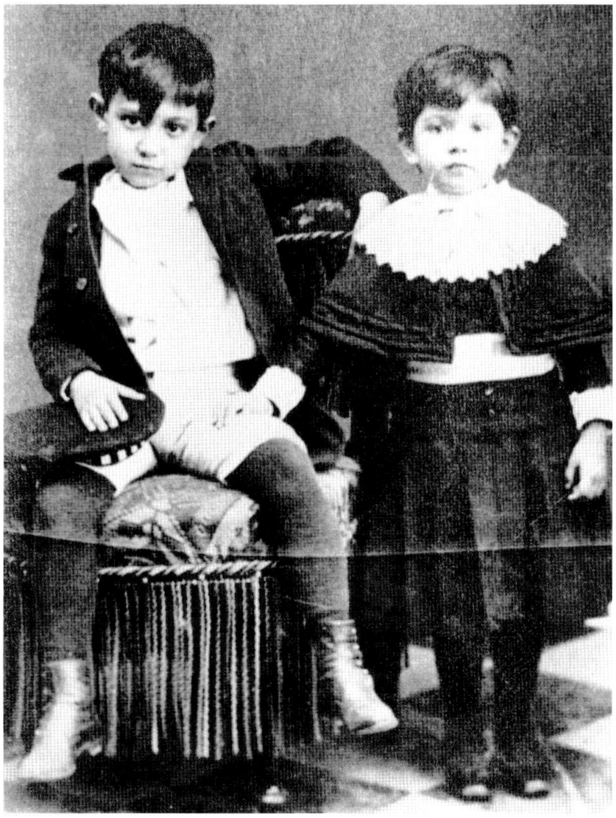

1899 Picasso returns to Barcelona. He mixes with avant-garde circles and frequents the Els Quatre Gats cabaret, where he meets Jaime Sabartès.

1900 First exhibition held at Els Quatre Gats. First visit to Paris, where he stays in Montmartre.

1901 Exhibition at the Galerie Ambroise Vollard. Picasso meets the poet Max Jacob. His friend Carlos Casagemas commits suicide. Beginning of the Blue Period.

1902 Spring and autumn exhibitions at the Galerie Berthe Weill.

1903 Returns to Barcelona in the spring.

1904 Back in Paris, Picasso takes a studio at the Bateau-Lavoir, Montmartre. Beginning of the Rose Period. Picasso meets Guillaume Apollinaire and commences his relationship with Fernande Olivier.

1905 Exhibition at the Galerie Serrurier. Meets Gertrude and Leo Stein.

1906 Picasso is introduced to Henri Matisse by Gertrude Stein. In the summer, he visits Gósol, in the Spanish Pyrenees, with Fernande Olivier.

1907 Begins working on *Les Demoiselles d'Avignon*. Picasso meets the collector Daniel-Henry Kahnweiler in the summer and Georges Braque in the autumn. A Paul Cézanne retrospective is held at the Paris Salon d'Automne.

1909 Picasso visits Horta de Ebro, Spain. In September, he moves to 11, Boulevard de Clichy, Paris (18th arrondissement). Sergei Diaghilev founds the Ballets Russes.

1911 Picasso does not exhibit at the Salon d'Automne. Eva Gouel enters his life.

1912 First collages and assemblages. First *papiers collées* in collaboration with Braque.

1913 Picasso's father dies in May. In the summer, the artist moves to a studio in the Rue Schoelcher, Paris (14th arrondissement).

1914 Picasso spends the summer in Avignon and returns to Paris at the end of November.

1915 Meets Jean Cocteau. Eva Gouel dies of tuberculosis.

1916 Picasso moves to Montrouge, on the southern outskirts of Paris.

1917 From February to April, Picasso tours Italy (Rome, Naples, Pompeii, Florence) while preparing the sets for Diaghilev's ballet *Parade*. He meets Olga Khokhlova. Returns to Paris at the end of April. *Parade* premières at the Théâtre de Châtelet, Paris, on 18 May. In June, Picasso visits Madrid, coming back to Paris in late November to live in Montrouge with Olga.

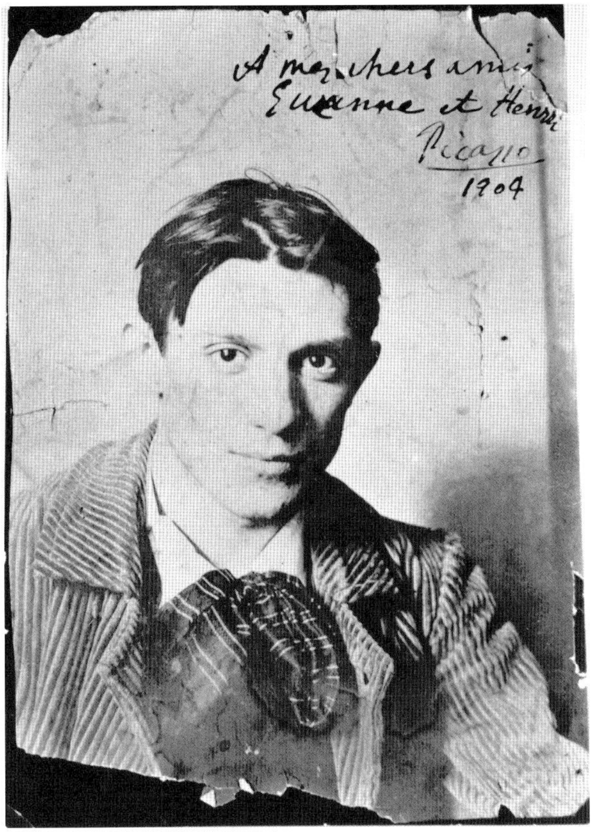

Picasso in Paris
1904

1918 Exhibition "Matisse-Picasso" at Paul Guillaume's in Paris. On 12 July, Picasso marries Olga at the Russian Church, in Paris. They spend the summer in Biarritz. In late November, the couple move to 23, Rue La Boétie, Paris (8th arrondissement). Apollinaire dies from Spanish influenza.

1919 Picasso visits England to work on the sets for the ballet *Tricorne*, performed at the Alhambra Theatre, London, on 22 July. Spends the summer with Olga in Saint-Raphaël, on the French Riviera.

1921 Birth of Picasso's first son, Paulo, on 4 February. On 22 May,

Cuadro Flamenco premières at the Théâtre de la Cigale, Paris, with sets designed by the artist. Spends the summer at Fontainebleau (where he paints *Three Women at the Spring*).

1922 Picasso spends the summer in Brittany (*Two Women Running on the Beach*).

1923 Picasso spends the summer on the French Riviera, at the Cap d'Antibes (*The Pipes of Pan*).

1924 The ballet *Mercure* premières at the Théâtre du Châtelet, Paris, on 18 June; the stage curtain was painted by Picasso. First performance of the ballet *Le Train Bleu* on 20 June. Picasso spends the summer in Juan-les-Pins, on the French Riviera. Publication of André Breton's *Premier Manifeste du surréalisme.* The first issue of the review *La Révolution surréaliste* is published in December.

1925 Picasso stays in Monte Carlo in March and April, then spends the summer in Juan-les-Pins. On 14 November, he takes part in the first exhibition of Surrealist painting at the Galerie Pierre, Paris. Death of Erik Satie. Paris hosts the International Exhibition of Decorative Arts.

1926 Christian Zervos launches the magazine *Les Cahiers d'art.*

1927 Picasso meets the 17-year-old Marie-Thérèse Walter.

1929 Second visit to Dinard, Brittany. Picasso makes the acquaintance of Salvador Dalí.

1930 Picasso purchases the Château

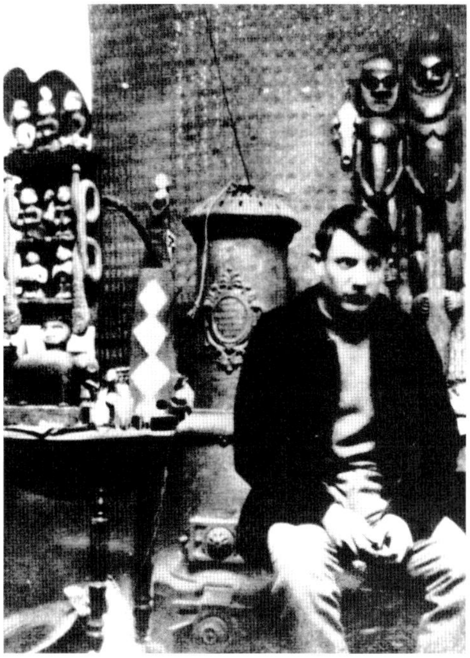

Picasso in his studio at the Bateau-Lavoir (photograph Gelett-Burgess), Paris, 1908

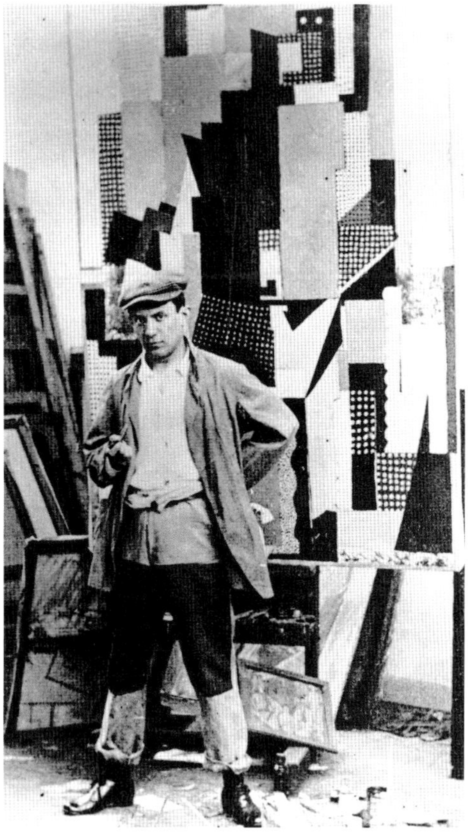

Self-portrait with *Man Leaning on a Table*
Paris, studio in Rue Schoelcher, 1914

de Boisgeloup, 80 km from Paris. In the autumn, Marie-Thérèse Walter moves into an apartment with Picasso on the Rue La Boétie, Paris.

1931 In May, he installs a sculpture studio at Boisgeloup.

1932 First retrospective exhibition held in June at the Galerie Georges Petit, Paris, and the Kunsthaus, Zurich.

1933 Surrealist exhibition at the Galerie Pierre Colle, Paris, features works by Duchamp, Éluard, Giacometti, Dalí, Magritte, Picasso, Man Ray and Tanguy. In June, the first issue of the magazine *Minotaure,* with cover by Picasso, is published by Albert Skira and E. Tériade.

1935 Exhibition of *papiers collés* at the Galerie Pierre. Picasso and Olga separate in June. Maya, Picasso and Marie-Thérèse's daughter is born on 5 September.

1936 Picasso's poetry is published in *Les Cahiers d'art.* He sees a great deal of Paul Éluard, who introduces him to Dora Maar, a painter and photographer. Picasso spends the summer at Mougins, in the French Alps, with Dora, the photographer Man Ray, the art dealer Paul Rosenberg, Paul Éluard and the publisher Christian Zervos. Picasso moves to Tremblay-sur-Mauldre, in the Parisian area, with Marie-Thérèse and Maya.

1937 Finds a new studio at 7, Rue des Grands-Augustins, Paris (6th arrondissement). On 26 April, General Franco, helped by German aviation, bombs the Basque town of Guernica.
On 12 July, the Spanish Pavilion at the Paris World Fair exhibits Picasso's mural *Guernica.*

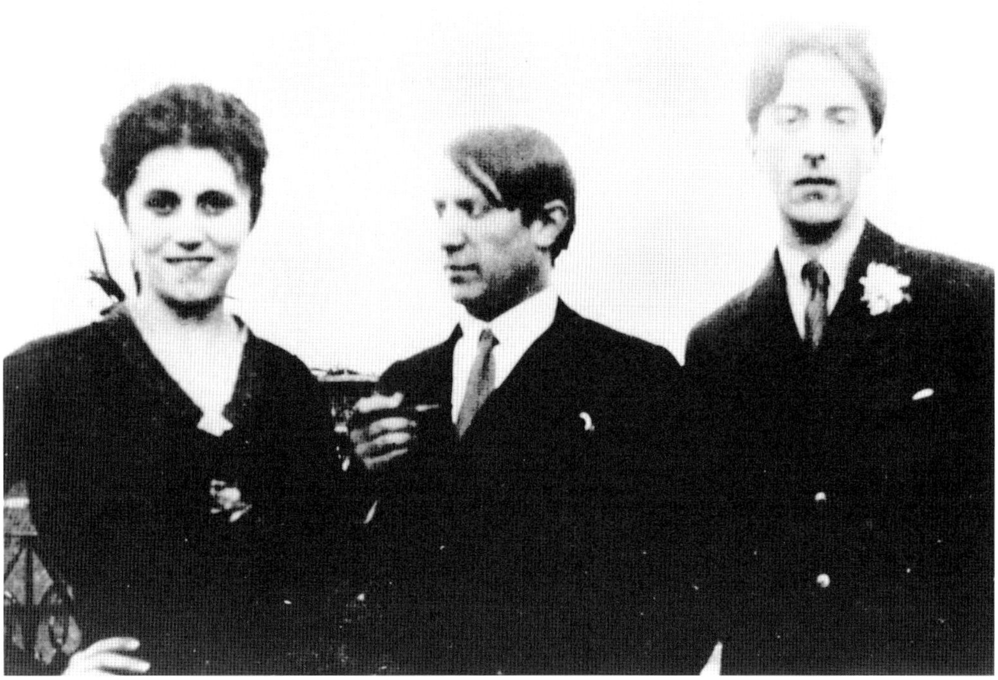

Olga Kokhlova,
Picasso and Jean Cocteau
Rome, 1917

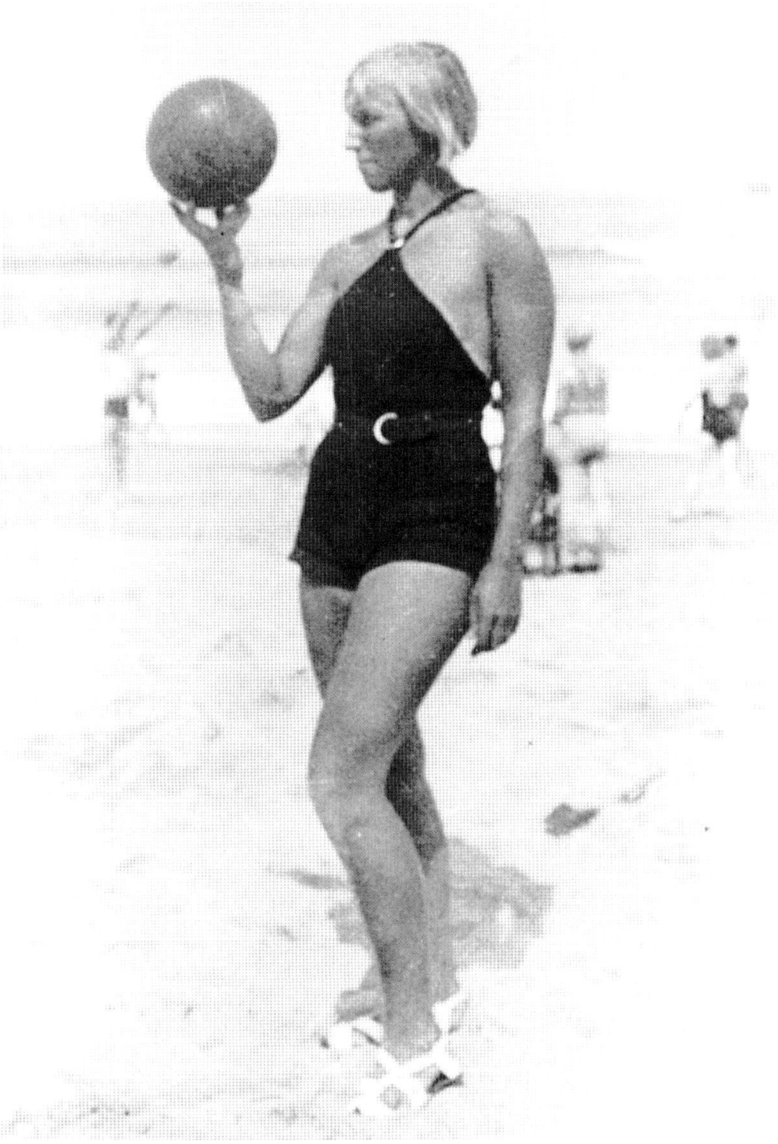

Picasso
Marie-Thérèse Walter
on the beach
Dinard, 1929

1939 Picasso's mother dies on 13 January, followed by the art dealer Ambroise Vollard on 22 July. Picasso visits Royan, on the Atlantic coast, several times. Retrospective exhibition entitled "Picasso: Forty Years of his Art" in New York.

1940 Picasso stays in Royan.

1941 Picasso writes the first Surrealist play, *Desire Caught by the Tail.*

1943 Picasso meets Françoise Gilot.

1944 Picasso joins the Communist Party on 5 October. The Paris Salon d'Automne and the Pablo Picasso retrospective open on 6 October.

1945 First lithographs produced in Fernand Mourlot's workshop in Paris. Picasso exhibits at the Salon d'Automne.

1946 Picasso and Françoise Gilot begin living together. From October to November, he works at the Château d'Antibes.

1947 Birth of Claude, son of Picasso and Françoise Gilot, on 15 May. Leaves for the Mediterranean resort of Golfe-Juan. In August, Picasso begins to make ceramics at the Ramié pottery, Vallauris.

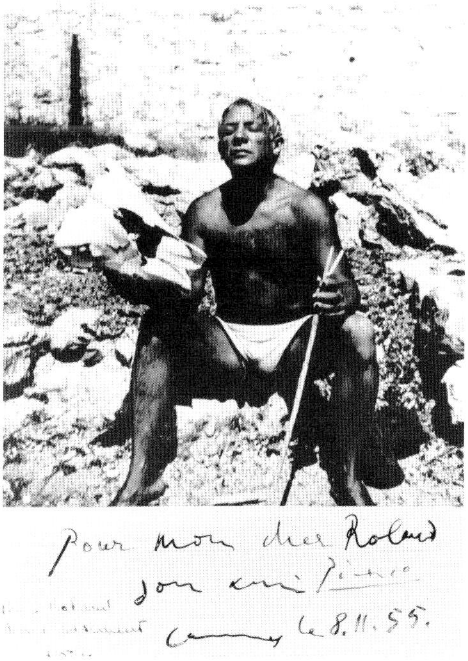

Dora Maar
Picasso with the skull
of a bovid
Juan-les-Pins, 1937

Death of the gallery owner Paul Rosenberg. Picasso writes his second play, *Four Little Girls*.

1948 24th Venice Biennale hosts the first exhibition of Picasso's works in Italy. He takes part in the World Congress of Intellectuals, in Wroclaw, Poland.

1949 Birth of Paloma, Picasso and Françoise's second child, on 19 April. Second visit to Italy for the Peace Congress in Rome.

1950 Picasso is awarded the Lenin Peace prize.

1952 Decorates the chapel of Vallauris with a fresco entitled *War and Peace*. Personal exhibition at the Galleria Nazionale d'Arte Moderna, Rome, and Palazzo Reale, Milan. Picasso does not go to Italy this year.

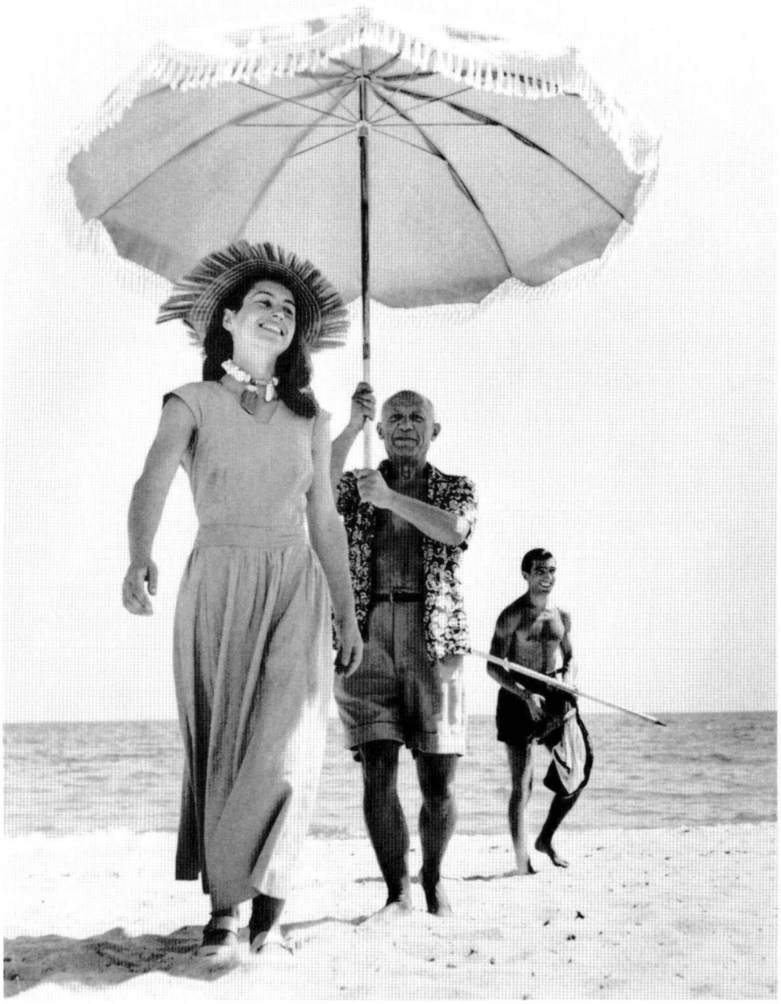

Robert Capa
Picasso holding a parasol on the beach with Françoise Gilot and Javier Vilato
Golfe-Juan, 1947

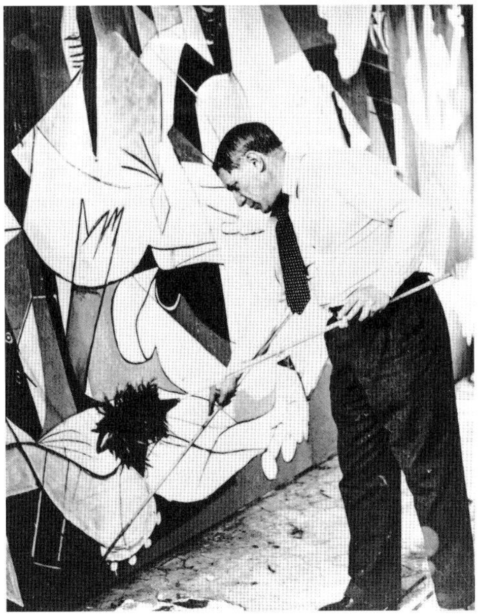

Dora Maar
Picasso painting *Guernica*
Paris, studio in the Rue des Grands-Augustins, 1937

1954 Picasso and Françoise Gilot separate. He leaves for Vallauris, then returns to Paris with Jacqueline Roque, whom he met in the Madoura studio, Vallauris. Death of Matisse.

1955 Death of Picasso's wife, Olga. In June, the artist moves into the villa "La Californie", Cannes, with Jacqueline. Retrospective exhibition at the Musée des Arts Décoratifs, Paris. Picasso works with Georges Clouzot on the film *Le Mystère Picasso*.

1956 Clouzot's film, *Le Mystère Picasso*, is released.

1957 Picasso paints *Las Meninas*, after Velázquez. Mural project for the UNESCO headquarters in Paris.

1958 Picasso buys the Château de Vauvenargues, at the foot of the Mont Sainte-Victoire, near Aix en-Provence.

1961 Picasso and Jacqueline Roque marry in Vallauris.

1963 Opening of the Museo Picasso, Barcelona. Braque dies on 31 August, followed by Cocteau on 11 October.

1966 Picasso retrospective at the Grand Palais and Petit Palais, Paris. Death of André Breton.

1967 Picasso leaves his studio in the Rue des Grands-Augustins, and refuses the Légion d'honneur.

1968 Death of his faithful friend and secretary, Sabartès.

1970 The artist's works that had remained in Picasso's family in Spain are donated to the Museo Picasso, Barcelona. Exhibition of recent works at the Papal Palace, Avignon.

1971 Picasso celebrates his 90th birthday.

1973 Exhibition of engravings from his late years at the Galerie Louise Leiris. Picasso dies at Mougins on 8 April. A vast anthological exhibition opens at the Papal Palace, Avignon, on 23 May.

David Douglas Duncan
Picasso and Jacqueline Roque in front of *Reclining Nude*
1958

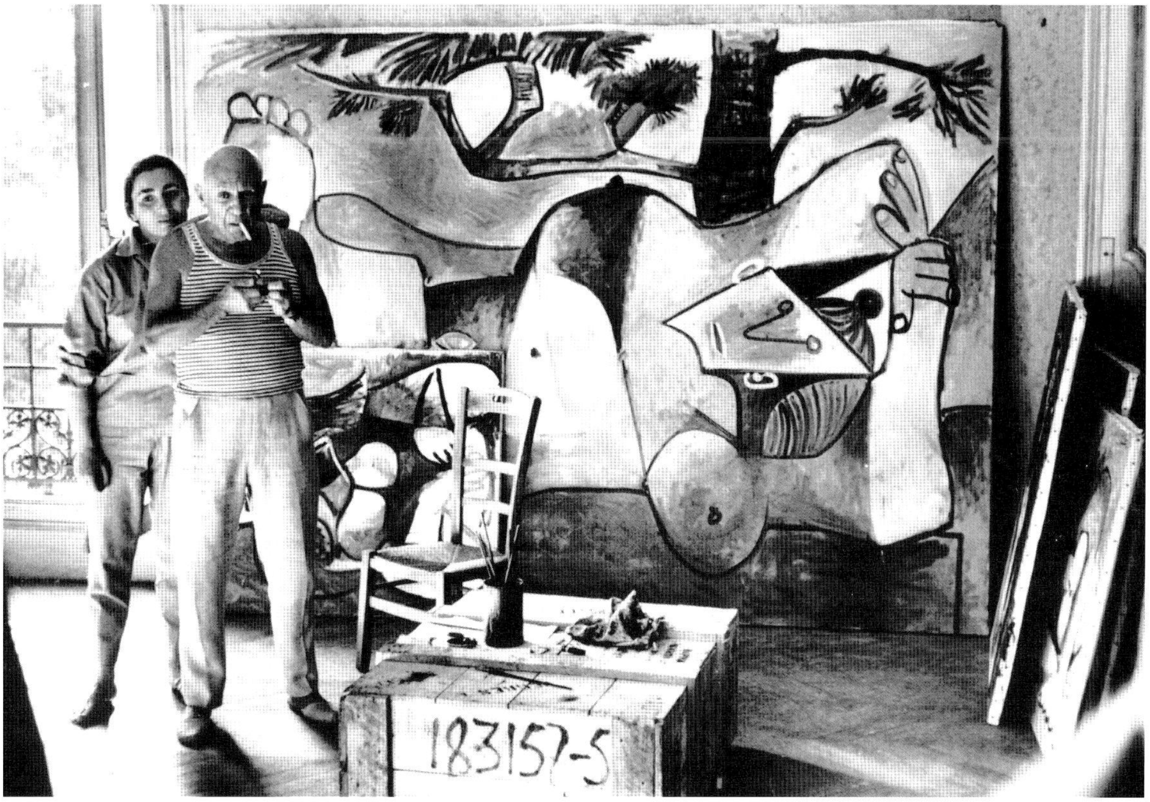

Selected Bibliography

Souvenirs and tributes

Bernadac, Marie-Laure, and Michael, Androula, *Picasso, propos sur l'art*, Paris, Gallimard, 1999

Brassaï, *Conversations avec Picasso*, Paris, Gallimard, 1964

Caizergues, Pierre, and Seckel, Hélène, *Picasso-Apollinaire. Correspondance*, Paris, Gallimard/Réunion des musées nationaux, 1992

Caws, Mary Ann, *Picasso's Weeping Woman: The Life and Art of Dora Maar*, London, Thames & Hudson, 2000

Duncan, David Douglas, *Le Petit Monde de Pablo Picasso*, Paris, Hachette, 1959

Duncan, David Douglas, *Goodbye Picasso*, New York, Gosset & Dunlap, 1974

Duncan, David Douglas, *The Silent Studio*, New York, Norton, 1976

Duncan, David Douglas, *Viva Picasso, a Centennial Celebration, 1881-1981*, New York, Viking Press, 1980

Éluard, Paul, *À Pablo Picasso*, Geneva, Les Trois Collines, 1944

Gilot, Françoise, and Lake, Carlton, *Life with Picasso*, New York, Doubleday, 1964

Kahnweiler, Daniel-Henry, *Mes galeries et mes peintres. Entretiens avec Francis Crémieux*, Paris, Gallimard, 1961.

Kahnweiler, Daniel-Henry, *Confessions esthétiques*, Paris, Gallimard, 1963

Laporte, Geneviève, *"Si tard le soir, le soleil brille". Pablo Picasso*, Paris, Plon, 1973

Malraux, André, *La Tête obsidienne*, Paris, Gallimard, 1974

Olivier, Fernande, *Picasso et ses amis*, Paris, Stock, 1933

Parmelin, Hélène, *Picasso sur la place*, Paris, Julliard, 1960

Parmelin, Hélène, *Picasso dit...* Paris, Gonthier, 1966

Parmelin, Hélène, *Voyage en Picasso*, Paris, Robert Laffont, 1980

Penrose, Roland, *Portrait of Picasso*, New York, The Museum of Modern Art, 1957

Sabartés, Jaime, *Pablo Picasso. Portraits et souvenirs*, Paris, Louis Carré and Maximilien Vox, 1946

Sabartés, Jaime, *Pablo Picasso. Documents iconographiques*, Geneva, Pierre Cailler, 1954

Monographs

Baldassari, Anne, *Picasso, Works on Paper*, Dublin, Merrell Publishers, 2000

Berger, John, *La Réussite et l'Échec de Picasso*, Paris, Denoël, 1968

Bernadac, Marie-Laure, et Du Bouchet, Paule, *Picasso le sage et le fou*, Paris, Gallimard, 1986

Cabanne, Pierre, *Le Siècle de Picasso*, two vols., Paris, Denoël, 1975

Clair, Jean, *Le Nu et la Norme: Klimt et Picasso, 1907*, Paris, Gallimard,1988

Daix, Pierre, *La Vie de peintre de Pablo Picasso*, Paris, Le Seuil, 1977

Daix, Pierre, *Picasso créateur*, Paris, Le Seuil, 1987

Fermigier, André, *Picasso*, Paris, Le Livre de Poche, 1969

Giraudy, Danièle, *Picasso. La mémoire du regard*, Paris, Cercle d'art, 1986

Gosselin, Gérard, *Picasso et la presse, un peintre dans l'histoire*, Paris, Cercle d'Art, 1999

Krauss, Rosalind, *The Picasso Papers*, London, Thames and Hudson, 1998

Léal, Brigitte, Piot, Christine, and Bernadac, Marie-Laure, *Picasso, la monographie*, Paris, Editions de la Martinière, 2001

Leymarie, Jean, *Picasso, métamorphoses et unité*, Geneva, Skira, 1971

McCully, Marilyn, *A Picasso Anthology: Documents, Criticism, Reminiscences*, London, Arts Council of Great Britain, 1981

Penrose, Roland, *Picasso 1881-1973*, London, Paul Eleck, 1973

Penrose, Roland, *Picasso*, Paris, Flammarion, 1982

Raynal, Maurice, *Picasso*, Geneva, Skira, 1953

Richardson, John, *A Life of Pablo Picasso*, vol. I, *1881-1906* ; vol. II, *1907-1917*, New York, Random House, 1991 and 1996

Schiff, Gert (ed.), *Picasso in Perspective*, Englewood Cliffs, Prentice Hall, 1976

Sollers, Philippe, *Picasso le héros*, Paris, Cercle d'art, 1999

Stein Gertrude, *Picasso*, Paris, Floury, 1938; 2nd edition, Paris, Christian Bourgois, 1978

Vallentin, Antonina, *Pablo Picasso*, Paris, Albin Michel, 1957

Reference books

Baer, Brigitte, *Picasso peintre-graveur*, Bern, Kornfeld, 1986-1990

Bernadac, Marie-Laure, and Piot, Christine, *Picasso. Écrits*, Paris, Réunion des musées

nationaux/Gallimard, 1989
Bloch, Georges and Picasso, Pablo, *Catalogue de l'œuvre gravé et lithographié*, Bern, Kornfeld & Klipstein, 1968-1979
Daix, Pierre, *Dictionnaire Picasso*, Paris, Laffont, Coll. Bouquins,1995
Daix, Pierre, and Boudaille, Georges, *Catalogue raisonné de l'œuvre peint*, Neuchâtel, Ides & Calendes, 1966
Daix, Pierre, and Rosselet, Joan, *Le Cubisme de Picasso. Catalogue raisonné de l'œuvre peint, 1907-1916*, Neuchâtel, Ides & Calendes, 1979
Duncan, David Douglas, *Les Picassos de Picasso*, Paris, Bibliothèque des Arts, 1961
Geiser, Bernhard, *Picasso peintre-graveur*, Bern, published by the author, 1933; reedited Bern, Kornfeld & Klipstein, 1968
Goeppert, Sebastian, Goeppert-Frank, Herma, and Cramer, Patrick, *Pablo Picasso. Catalogue raisonné des livres illustrés*, Geneva, Patrick Cramer, 1983
Mourlot, Fernand, *Picasso lithographe*, four vols., Monte-Carlo, André Sauret, 1949-1964
Palau i Fabre, Josep, *Picasso vivant (1881-1907)*, Paris, Albin Michel, 1981
Palau i Fabre, Josep, *Picasso cubisme, 1907-1917*, Paris, Albin Michel, 1990
Palau i Fabre, Josep, *Picasso 1917-1926, des ballets au drame*, Cologne, Könemann, 1999
Ramié, Georges, *Céramique de Picasso*, Paris, Cercle d'art, 1974
Spies, Werner, *Picasso. Das Plastische Werk* (catalogue of sculptures in collaboration with Christine Piot), Stuttgart, Gerd Hatje, 1983
Spies, Werner, *Picasso sculpteur*, Paris, Éditions du Centre Georges Pompidou, 2000
Zervos, Christian, *Pablo Picasso, Les Cahiers d'art*, vol. I-XXXIII, 1932-1978

Exhibition catalogues

Picasso, œuvres reçues en paiement des droits de succession, Paris, Grand Palais, 1979-1980
Pablo Picasso, A Retrospective, New York, The Museum of Modern Art, 1930
Babelon, Jean-Pierre, *Petit guide du musée Picasso: l'hôtel Salé*, Paris, Réunion des musées nationaux, new edition (available in English), 1999
Baldassari, Anne, *Picasso photographe 1901-1916*, Paris, Réunion des musées nationaux, 1994
Baldassari, Anne, *Picasso et la photographie*, Paris, Réunion des musées nationaux, 1995
Baldassari, Anne, *Le Miroir noir. Picasso, sources photographiques 1900-1928*, Paris, Réunion des musées nationaux, 1997
Baldassari, Anne, *Brassaï/Picasso. Conversations avec la lumière*, Paris, Réunion des musées nationaux, 2000
Baldassari, Anne, Dupuis-Labbé, Dominique, Giraudon, Colette, Léal, Brigitte, and Seckel, Hélène, *L'ABCdaire de Picasso*, Paris, Réunion des musées nationaux/Flammarion, 1996
Bernadac, Marie-Laure, *Le Dernier Picasso*, Paris, Éditions du Centre Georges Pompidou, 1988
Bernadac, Marie-Laure, and Breteau, Giselle, *Picasso à l'écran*, Paris, Réunion des musées nationaux/ Éditions du Centre Georges Pompidou, 1992
Bernadac, Marie-Laure, and Léal, Brigitte, *Picasso: Toros y Toreros*, Paris, Réunion des musées nationaux, 1993
Léal, Brigitte, *Picasso: jeunesse et genèse. Dessins 1895-1905*, Paris, Réunion des musées nationaux, 1991
Léal, Brigitte, *Musée Picasso, carnets, catalogue des dessins*, Paris, Réunion des musées nationaux, 1996
Léal, Brigitte, *Papiers collés*, Paris, Réunion des musées nationaux, 1998
Régnier, Gérard, *Corps crucifiés*, Paris, Réunion des musées nationaux, 1993
Régnier, Gérard, *Picasso érotique*, Paris, Réunion des musées nationaux, 2001
Rubin, William, *Picasso-Braque: Pioneering Cubism*, New York, The Museum of Modern Art, 1989
Seckel, Hélène, *Les Demoiselles d'Avignon*, Paris, Musée Picasso, 1988
Seckel, Hélène, *Max Jacob et Picasso*, Paris, Réunion des musées nationaux, 1994
Seckel-Klein, Hélène, *Picasso collectionneur*, Paris, Réunion des musées nationaux, 1998

Guidebooks

Catalogue sommaire du musée Picasso. vol I: *Peintures, sculptures, céramiques, collection personnelle*, 1985; vol II: *Dessins, aquarelles, gouaches et pastels*, 1987; vol III: *Carnets de dessins*, vol. I and II, Paris, Réunion des musées nationaux,1996
Seckel, Hélène, *Musée Picasso, Visitor's Guide*, Paris, Réunion des musées nationaux,1985

Photographic credits

Réunion des musées nationaux, Paris:
Franck Raux (p. 9, 97); Béatrice Hatala (p. 11, 25, 29, 49, 55, 61, 64, 87, 88-89, 95, 99); R-G Ojeda (p. 13, 15, 17 and cover, 19, 21,23, 27, 35, 47, 53, 57, 59, 63, 65, 67, 71); J-G Berizzi p. 31, 33, 37, 39, 41, 43, 45, 51, 73, 77, 79, 81, 83, 85, 91, 93, 101, 105, 107, 109, 111, 113, 115).
Archives of the Musée Picasso
p. 118, 120, 121; Gelett-Burgess (p. 119); Picasso (p. 119); Dora Maar (p. 121, 122); Robert Capa (p. 122); David Douglas Duncan (p. 123).

Published by the Réunion des Musées Nationaux Publications
Department under the direction of Béatrice Foulon

Coordinating editor:
Bernadette Caille

Cover design:
Gilles Huot/H.D.L. Design

Graphic design and layout:
Cécile Neuville

Text edited by:
Julie Houis

Translation:
Pamela Hargreaves

Picture research:
Caroline de Lambertye
Marie-Josée Lecoeur

Production:
Jacques Venelli

Photoengraving:
GEGM

This book was printed and bound
by the Imprimerie Kapp Lahure Jombart

Dépôt légal: March 2002
ISBN: 2-7118-4252-5
GA: 20 4252